BUONGIORNO!

Breakfast and Brunch, Italian Style

Norman Kolpas

Photography by Chris Cassidy

CB

CONTEMPORARY BOOKS

Library of Congress Cataloging-in-Publication Data

Kolpas, Norman.
     Buongiorno! : breakfast and brunch, Italian style / Norman Kolpas.
        p.   cm.
     ISBN 0-8092-9733-7
     1. Breakfasts.   2. Brunches.   3. Cookery, Italian.   I. Title.

TX733 .K6525   2001
641.5′2—dc21

                                       00-59014

Featured on the cover: Lemon Ricotta Pancakes with Quick Raspberry Compote (see page 64)

Interior design by Kim Bartko
Interior photography by Chris Cassidy
Interior illustration by Todd Petersen

Published by Contemporary Books
A division of NTC/Contemporary Publishing Group, Inc.
4255 West Touhy Avenue, Lincolnwood (Chicago), Illinois 60712-1975 U.S.A.
Copyright © 2001 by Norman Kolpas
Printed at Midas Printing Ltd., Hong Kong
International Standard Book Number: 0-8092-9733-7
18   17   16   15   14   13   12   11   10   9   8   7   6   5   4   3   2   1

CONTENTS

INTRODUCTION

Breakfast pasta tossed with scrambled eggs, prosciutto, Parmesan, and a touch of garlic. Custardy French toast made with panettone, the rich Italian dried-fruit bread. Bowls of polenta, the Italian cornmeal porridge, topped with brown sugar and melting lumps of sweet butter. Creamy risotto made from Arborio rice, cooked and chilled as a sweet pudding. Baked eggs nested in beds of chunky, well-seasoned tomato sauce. Frittatas, flat omelets abounding with vegetables and cheeses. Steaming cups of espresso, cappuccino, and caffe latte. Such dishes, and so many more, can make breakfast or brunch almost as stimulating an experience as a trip to Tuscany, Venice, or Rome.

That's the philosophy behind *Buongiorno!* The 100 recipes on the following pages have been created expressly to feature beloved Italian ingredients and capture favorite Italian flavors, promising a "Good morning!" centered around the breakfast or brunch table.

If you've ever traveled in Italy, you know that breakfast is, in fact, not a big meal there. Most Italians start their day with milk-laced espresso, some crusty bread with jam, and maybe some cold cuts. Leave it to Americans, however, to take dishes Italians might serve for a light luncheon, dinner, or dessert and transform them into exciting specialties for the breakfast or brunch table. Just such a vital trend is going on all over the nation, at upscale restaurants and casual cafés in San Francisco, New York, Dallas, Chicago, Los Angeles, Kansas City, Seattle, Providence, and other cities and towns everywhere.

Such Italian-inspired dishes translate easily to the home kitchen. After all, they're variations on the things we already love to eat for breakfast: eggs, quick breads, pancakes and French toast, breakfast meats, cereals, and fresh fruit. Those very clear-cut categories provide the basic chapter divisions into which this book's recipes are organized.

The widespread popularity of Italian cooking puts any special ingredients you might need within easy reach. Following this Introduction, you'll find a glossary of the most frequently recurring ingredients, along with basic recipes called for repeatedly throughout the book. If you have a well-stocked supermarket, specialty foods store, or Italian deli within easy driving distance, shopping should be a cinch.

A NOTE ON PLANNING MENUS

Even a single recipe from this book—be it Lemon Ricotta Pancakes with Quick Raspberry Compote; Linguine with Smoked Salmon, Scrambled Eggs, Lemon Zest, and Chives; Panettone-Style Scones; or Peaches in Red Wine (see Index)—can set a delightful Italian-style tone for a morning meal. So don't feel that you must go all out and prepare a five-course menu to make a breakfast or brunch special.

That said, the recipes have been designed to make it as easy as possible for you to prepare as simple or elaborate a breakfast or brunch as you might like. Most of them easily divide into smaller yields or double or triple for larger gatherings. A majority of the recipes may be quickly prepared; those that are more involved include tips for making them partially or entirely in advance.

Plan your menus according to the season and weather, to the style of the occasion, to your knowledge of guests' tastes, and to how much time you have. Serve lighter dishes on warmer summer mornings, more robust and hot recipes when there's a chill in the air. Aim to balance the menu as you would for any breakfast or brunch—accompanying egg dishes (or pasta-egg combinations) with a special bread or breakfast meat, for example, or offering a fresh fruit dish to start or end the meal. Many of the introductory notes to individual recipes include such serving suggestions.

Always bear in mind, too, that any entertaining you do should by rights be as much of a pleasure for you as it is for your guests. One or two recipes prepared by you at leisure and served with ease will always be more pleasurable for everyone than an elaborate menu that keeps you from spending time with your guests.

GLOSSARY OF ITALIAN INGREDIENTS AND BASIC RECIPES

All of the ingredients called for in the recipes in this book can be found in well-stocked supermarkets, Italian delicatessens, or specialty foods stores. To keep your shopping time to a minimum, search for them in that order, particularly because most upscale supermarkets today carry extensive selections of Italian cold cuts and cheeses in their deli departments.

AMARETTI

These crisp, light little cookies are flavored with the bitter almonds that give them their name. They are widely available under the Lazzaroni di Saronno brand, with the round cookies enclosed in pairs in tissue wrappers and sealed inside a red-and-orange tin. Although they may be crumbled to lend body to desserts or sweet fillings, amaretti are most often enjoyed with a cup of coffee and are wonderful to serve at the end of a break-fast or brunch.

AMARETTO

This sweet straw-colored liqueur is flavored with bitter almonds and apricots. Very popu-lar and widely available, it can be used as a flavoring for baked goods or fruits or added to or enjoyed alongside coffee.

BALSAMIC VINEGAR

Unlike most vinegars, which are made from wines, this specialty of Italy's Modena region is based on the juice of white grapes that is boiled down to concentrate it and then aged for many years in ever-smaller barrels made from different woods that add their own unique flavors to the vinegar. Powerful and syrupy, with a pleasing edge of sweetness and a complex taste, balsamic vinegar is sometimes even sipped as a cordial. More often, however, it is used in dressings or as a flavoring that can even complement fresh fruit. Look for true balsamic vinegar imported from Italy, in bottles that indicate it comes from Modena and has been aged for a specified number of years. It can be costly, but a little goes a long way and tastes far superior to more generic and less expensive, thinner balsamic-flavored vinegars.

Bell Peppers, Roasted

Roasting bell peppers serves three different, highly desirable purposes. It makes the flesh of a pepper tender and supple. It develops a pepper's natural sweetness. And it makes it possible to remove the pepper's shiny, indigestible skin.

To roast one or more peppers, place them on their sides on a foil-lined baking sheet under a hot broiler. As the skins begin to blister, turn the peppers; continue turning them until their skins are evenly blistered and blackened all over. Loosely close the foil around the peppers to help them steam as they cool; this will further loosen their skins.

When the peppers are cool enough to handle, peel off the skins with your fingertips. Pull out the stem ends and slit the peppers open, taking care to avoid any hot steam from inside. Discard the stems and seeds. Use the tip of a small sharp knife to cut out any white ribs and attached seeds, and pick up any stray seeds with the tip of a small spoon.

Some recipes may call for the peppers drained of their juices. Transfer the peppers to a fine-meshed strainer and let the juices drip into a bowl, reserving them as a flavoring for a dressing or sauce.

Bread

For authentic Italian breakfast toast, seek out a bakery that produces rustic peasant-style Italian or French loaves. Barring that, a good-quality sourdough loaf will do nicely.

Cheeses

The eight different classic Italian cheeses called for throughout this book are relatively easy to find. Nevertheless, seek out the best-quality products you can find to enjoy each cheese's unique and true characteristics.

ASIAGO This cow's-milk cheese of northeastern Italy resembles a fine cheddar when young and takes on a sharper flavor and firmer consistency suitable for grating when aged for one to two years.

FONTINA From the Val d'Aosta in northwestern Italy, this rich, dense-textured cow's-milk cheese has a creamy, earthy taste. Look for a true imported fontina rather than blander fontina-style cheeses made in the United States, France, or Scandinavia.

GORGONZOLA A specialty of the Milan-area town of the same name, this cow's-milk cheese develops greenish blue veins that give it a tangy, spicy flavor that counterpoints its richness.

MASCARPONE This spreadable cheese is made by lightly souring cream, which gives it a tangy edge that complements its very rich taste and consistency. French crème fraîche or Mexican crema may be substituted.

MOZZARELLA This familiar stringy white cheese, traditionally made from water-buffalo milk but now just as likely from cow's milk, has a mild flavor and soft, chewy consistency that make it a favorite eaten in salads or melted in egg dishes or on top of pizzas. Fresh mozzarella, sold still floating in its watery whey, is especially mild and smooth. Good-quality commercially packaged mozzarellas, less moist and denser in consistency, are better suited to cooking.

PARMESAN The best examples of this golden, well-aged cow's-milk cheese with a distinctively nutty, tangy flavor come from Italy's Emilia-Romagna region and are labeled Parmigiano-Reggiano, which is stenciled on the rinds of the big wheels in which they are produced. Don't settle for domestic Parmesan or those made in other countries. For the best flavor and texture, buy Parmesan by the wedge or block, cut from the large wheel, and grate or shave it freshly just before use.

PROVOLONE Mild tasting, yet packing a nutty bite of flavor, this cow's-milk cheese from southern Italy has a smooth texture and is usually formed into large salami-like shapes that yield circular slices.

RICOTTA The name, which literally means "recooked," refers to the process by which this mild, fresh, fluffy-textured white cheese is made. The milky whey left over from the making of other cow's-milk cheeses like mozzarella and provolone is reprocessed to produce ricotta, which becomes the basis for many fillings and can also lend lightness to eggs or pancake batters. Packed in plastic tubs, ricotta is available in whole-milk, low-fat, and nonfat varieties, which vary correspondingly in richness.

Whipped Mascarpone Cream

The addition of mascarpone brings distinctive tang to this whipped cream, which is an ideal topping for morning fruit dishes. Do not whip the cream too far in advance; it will hold well in the refrigerator for several hours but no longer.

MAKES ABOUT 2 CUPS

¾ cup heavy cream, well chilled
¼ cup mascarpone, at room temperature

2 tablespoons confectioners' sugar

Chill a mixing bowl and clean beaters in the freezer for about 10 minutes.

Pour the cream into the chilled bowl. Insert the chilled beaters into the electric mixer and beat at medium to high speed until the cream begins to thicken noticeably but is still fairly fluid. Add the mascarpone and sugar and continue beating until the mixture forms soft, droopy peaks when the beaters are lifted out. Be careful not to overbeat. Cover and refrigerate until serving time.

EGGS AND EGG SUBSTITUTES

I used extra-large eggs when testing recipes for this book. Feel free to substitute low-fat or nonfat commercial egg products, found in the supermarket's refrigerated or freezer cases, in any of the egg or pasta dishes; follow the manufacturer's suggested quantities.

FRANGELICO

Wild hazelnuts and herbs provide the flavor for this brand-name liqueur, which can add enticing hazelnut flavor to baked goods or other cooked dishes or be sipped alongside or added to coffee.

Herbs

Many fresh and dried herbs bring variety to the Italian kitchen. Those best suited to the morning table follow.

Basil   Use this relative of mint fresh, the better to enjoy its bright, peppery aroma and flavor. To cut it into thin shreds, roll up a stack of leaves lengthwise and then cut the roll crosswise with a small, sharp knife.

Italian Parsley   This is the common name for the flat-leafed version of the popular, fresh-tasting kitchen herb, which has noticeably more flavor than the curly-leafed type typically used as a garnish.

Oregano   This pungent herb is one of the rare ones that actually gains and improves in flavor with drying. Crumble dried oregano with your fingertips before use to release more of its flavor.

Marsala

This fortified wine from Sicily is made in both sweet and less-common dry styles. To flavor breakfast or brunch baked goods or fruits, look for a good-quality imported sweet marsala.

Olive Oil

Not so long ago the merits of olive oil had to be explained carefully to cooks who didn't live in Mediterranean lands. Now we know how good the flavor of olive oil can be when it is extracted from the fruit of the olive tree by a first cold pressing, without use of heat or chemicals, to produce the product known as *extra-virgin olive oil*. Like wines, olive oils vary in color and flavor depending on where and precisely how they were produced and from what kinds of olives. Many specialty foods stores today will let you sample some of the olive oils they have for sale so you can find one that best suits your taste.

Oranges, Blood

In season from late winter into late spring, these flavorful, aromatic oranges have flesh tinged a deep orange-red, a color betrayed by the blush of red on their orange skins. A specialty grown in northern Sicily, this dramatic-looking fruit is prized throughout Italy.

PANCETTA

This Italian unsmoked bacon is made from the pork belly, cured with salt, black peppers, and sometimes other spices and rolled up into a tight cylinder that, when thinly sliced, yields pinwheels. Rich yet mild, pancetta is most often used chopped as a flavoring.

PANETTONE

This cylindrical loaf of egg-enriched bread studded with dried fruit is widely sold in Italian delicatessens and some well-stocked supermarkets and specialty foods stores, most often as commercial products sealed airtight to preserve their freshness and packed in decorative boxes. Enjoy it sliced and toasted or as the basis for French toast.

PASTRY, BASIC TART

For savory quiches and sweet fruit tarts alike, use this basic, easily made pastry. Or feel free to substitute good-quality frozen pastry dough or preformed shells from the market.

Basic Tart Pastry

MAKES 1 9-INCH TART SHELL

1½ cups all-purpose flour
½ teaspoon salt

½ cup unsalted butter, chilled and
cut into ½-inch cubes
3 to 4 tablespoons cold water

Put the flour and salt in a food processor fitted with the metal blade. Pulse the machine a few times to combine them. Add the butter and pulse several times, just until the mixture resembles coarse crumbs. Next, add 1 tablespoon of the water and pulse briefly; then, 1 tablespoon at a time, add only enough water for the dough to come together in a rough mass.

With floured hands, and taking care not to touch the sharp edges of the metal blade, transfer the dough from the bowl to a floured work surface. Pat the dough into a smooth, evenly circular disk about 1 inch thick. Use the dough immediately or wrap it securely in plastic wrap and refrigerate for up to 2 days (or wrap airtight and freeze for up to 2 months, defrosting in the refrigerator before use).

PESTO

This signature sauce of Genoa is made by pulverizing together fresh basil, garlic, pine nuts, Parmesan cheese, and olive oil. It makes a wonderful filling for omelets or a sauce for breakfast pizzas. While you can buy small jars of pesto in Italian delis and well-stocked markets, and can often find containers of more freshly made pesto in supermarket refrigerated cases close to the fresh pasta, nothing beats pesto you make yourself. I've relied on the following quick and easy version of the classic sauce since I developed it for my cookbook *Pasta Presto*. Many buyers of that book say it has become their own standard recipe. Because some people might not want too heavy a dose of garlic in the morning, I've provided a range here; use less or more as you wish. If you have pesto left over, put it in a nonreactive container, smooth its surface level, and cover with a film of olive oil before covering with plastic wrap and refrigerating for 3 or 4 days. Stir in the oil before using.

Basic Pesto

MAKES ABOUT 2 CUPS

6 tablespoons pine nuts

1½ cups packed fresh basil leaves

¾ cup extra-virgin olive oil

½ cup freshly grated Parmesan cheese

½ to 2 medium-size garlic cloves

Preheat the oven to 325°F. Spread the pine nuts in a single layer on a baking sheet, put them in the oven, and toast them until light golden, 7 to 10 minutes, watching them carefully and stirring occasionally to guard against burning. Remove from the oven and let them cool briefly, during which time they will continue to darken slightly in color.

Put the pine nuts and all the remaining ingredients, including garlic to taste, in a food processor fitted with the metal blade. Pulse the machine several times until the ingredients are coarsely chopped. Scrape down the work bowl. Then process continuously until the pesto is smooth.

PINE NUTS

The small, cylindrical seeds of a species of pine tree, these ivory-colored nuts have a rich, resinous flavor evocative of the Mediterranean. Use them as a garnish for sweet or savory breakfast dishes. Store pine nuts in the freezer in an airtight bag to preserve their freshness.

PIZZA DOUGH

The foundation for pizzas, in the morning as well as at other times of day, is a basic yeast-leavened bread dough. Use either of the following dough recipes as the basis for any of the breakfast pizzas in this book. Alternatively, look for a good ready-to-bake frozen bread dough. Or, as a shortcut, substitute prebaked pizza bread shells such as those sold under the Boboli label.

White Pizza Dough

This recipe yields the kind of thin, crisp crust favored nowadays for California-style pizzas.

MAKES ABOUT 1½ POUNDS DOUGH; 4 SERVINGS

1 ¼-ounce envelope active dry yeast	3 cups all-purpose flour
2 teaspoons sugar	1 teaspoon salt
1½ cups lukewarm water	3 tablespoons extra-virgin olive oil

In a small bowl, combine the yeast and 1 teaspoon of the sugar. Add ½ cup of the lukewarm water and stir until the yeast and sugar dissolve. Set aside until the yeast begins to foam, 3 to 5 minutes.

To mix the dough in a food processor fitted with the metal blade, put the flour, salt, and remaining sugar in the work bowl and pulse the machine several times to blend them. With the motor running, pour in the yeast mixture and the oil through the feed tube, then gradually pour in enough of the remaining water to form a smooth dough. ➤

Continue processing just until the dough forms a ball that rides around the bowl on the blade, a sign that the dough is sufficiently kneaded.

To mix the dough by hand, stir together the flour, salt, and remaining sugar in a large mixing bowl. Make a well in the center. Add the yeast mixture, oil, and remaining water and gradually stir from the center outward until the ingredients come together to form a soft, sticky dough. Transfer the dough to a floured work surface and knead by pushing down and away on its center with the heel of your hand, then gathering it back together, giving it a quarter turn, and repeating. If the dough is too sticky, sprinkle on more flour. Continue kneading until it is smooth and elastic, 5 to 7 minutes.

Oil a bowl with olive oil or coat it with nonstick spray and transfer the dough to it. Cover with a damp kitchen towel and leave it at room temperature to rise until doubled in bulk, 1 to 2 hours; or let it rise more slowly in the refrigerator for several hours or overnight.

Remove the dough from the bowl and cut it into four equal pieces. The dough is ready to shape and bake.

To freeze the dough, wrap each ball airtight in plastic wrap or a zippered plastic bag and place in the freezer, where it will keep for several weeks. Defrost at room temperature for 2 to 3 hours or overnight in the refrigerator before making pizzas.

Whole Wheat Pizza Dough

If you're the sort who prefers more robust whole wheat bread in the morning, this pizza dough is for you.

MAKES ABOUT 1½ POUNDS DOUGH; 4 SERVINGS

1 ¼-ounce envelope active dry yeast	2 cups all-purpose flour
2 teaspoons honey	1 cup whole wheat flour
1½ cups lukewarm water	1 teaspoon sea salt
	3 tablespoons extra-virgin olive oil

In a small bowl, combine the yeast and 1 teaspoon of the honey. Add ½ cup of the lukewarm water and stir until the yeast and honey dissolve. Set aside until the yeast begins to foam, 3 to 5 minutes.

To mix the dough in a food processor fitted with the metal blade, put both flours and the salt in the work bowl and pulse the machine several times to blend them. With the motor running, pour in the yeast mixture, the remaining honey, and the oil through the feed tube, then gradually pour in enough of the remaining water to form a smooth dough. Continue processing just until the dough forms a ball that rides around the bowl on the blade, a sign that the dough is sufficiently kneaded.

To mix the dough by hand, stir together both flours and the salt in a large mixing bowl. Make a well in the center. Add the yeast mixture, oil, and remaining honey and water and gradually stir from the center outward until the ingredients come together to form a soft, sticky dough. Transfer the dough to a floured work surface and knead the dough by pushing down and away on its center with the heel of your hand, then gathering it back together, giving it a quarter turn, and repeating. If the dough is too sticky, sprinkle on more flour. Continue kneading until it is smooth and elastic, 5 to 7 minutes.

Oil a bowl with olive oil or coat it with nonstick spray and transfer the dough to it. Cover with a damp kitchen towel and leave it at room temperature to rise until doubled in bulk, 1 to 2 hours; or let it rise more slowly in the refrigerator for several hours or overnight.

Remove the dough from the bowl and cut it into four equal pieces. The dough is ready to shape and bake.

To freeze the dough, wrap each ball airtight in plastic wrap or a zippered plastic bag and place in the freezer, where it will keep for several weeks. Defrost at room temperature for 2 to 3 hours or overnight in the refrigerator before making pizzas.

POLENTA

The term refers both to Italian ground cornmeal and to the thick porridge cooked from it. When making polenta from scratch, the best flavor and texture come from using coarsely ground cornmeal imported from Italy. Use quick-cooking or instant polenta, a finer-textured product made from precooked and redried grains, in baked goods or for griddle cakes that benefit from its softer consistency when cooked. If you are pressed for time and want to make one of the baked or broiled polenta recipes, which require cooking polenta and then cooling, molding, and cutting it, look instead for some of the excellent vacuum-packed plastic tubes of precooked polenta, ready to slice and prepare.

PROSCIUTTO

The rich taste of this raw, dry-cured Italian ham, a specialty of Parma and other northern regions, comes from feeding hogs on the whey left over from making Parmesan cheese. Thinly sliced prosciutto, with its salty-sweet flavor and supple, velvety texture, may be savored on its own, combined with sweet, juicy fruit, or used as a seasoning in morning egg or pasta dishes.

RICE

Italians use a short, plump-grained variety of rice to make their signature risotto dishes, which develop a creamy sauce during cooking thanks to the surface starch that dissolves from the grains. The three most common varieties of rice used for risotto are Arborio, Carnaroli, and Vialone Nano; the first two yield the creamiest results.

SAUSAGES

Two types of Italian fresh pork sausages are usually sold: so-called sweet sausages, usually seasoned with fennel seeds; and spicy sausages spiked with flakes of crushed chile. Many butchers now also offer Italian-style sausages made with turkey or chicken, to appeal to health-conscious customers. When selecting a breakfast sausage, go with whichever type better suits your palate; consider buying a selection so you can offer your guests a choice.

To cook fresh Italian sausages, puncture each one in two or three places with a fork. Put them in a saucepan, cover with cold water, and bring to a boil over medium heat; this will ensure that the sausages are cooked through. Then finish off the sausages in a nonstick skillet or under a hot broiler until they are browned uniformly.

TOMATOES

Tomatoes are such an integral part of Italian cooking that it's hard to imagine they didn't find their way to Italy until well into the sixteenth century, after Columbus brought them back to Europe from the New World. On the Italian-style breakfast table, they appear in the form of fresh tomatoes such as the always reliable Roma (plum) variety; as sun-dried tomatoes, intensely chewy and flavorful morsels that gain in flavor and texture from being packed in olive oil; as double-concentrate tomato paste, packed in squeeze tubes—available in well-stocked markets, specialty food stores, and Italian delis—and ready to intensify the flavor of a sauce; and as canned tomatoes, of which the best are generally considered to be imported Italian plum tomatoes of the San Marzano variety.

Basic Tomato Sauce

Use this as a basic sauce for the recipes in this book that call for a quick, flavorful Italian-style tomato sauce. For some recipes, such as the Three-Cheese Lasagna (see Index), you may have to double the quantities. If you'd like a chunkier sauce, substitute canned diced tomatoes for the crushed tomatoes. Stored airtight, any leftover sauce keeps well in the refrigerator for up to 1 week or in the freezer for 2 to 3 months.

MAKES ABOUT 3 CUPS

- 2 tablespoons extra-virgin olive oil
- 2 garlic cloves, pressed through a garlic press
- 2 shallots or ½ small onion, cut into chunks and pressed through a garlic press
- 1 28-ounce can crushed Italian tomatoes
- 1 tablespoon sugar
- ½ tablespoon dried oregano, crumbled
- ½ tablespoon dried basil, crumbled
- ¾ teaspoon salt
- 2 bay leaves

In a medium saucepan, heat the olive oil over medium heat. Add the garlic and shallots or onion and sauté until fragrant, 3 to 5 minutes. Stir in the remaining ingredients, reduce the heat to low, and simmer, stirring frequently, until thick, about 30 minutes.

Vin Santo

Made from dried grapes, this central-Italian dessert wine has an intense, nutlike, fruity flavor that can be used as an enhancement for fruit dishes destined for the morning table.

Wine, Sparkling

A glass or two of sparkling wine makes a wonderful festive addition to a special weekend breakfast, whether sipped on its own or as part of a cocktail such as those in Chapter 1. Most people consider slightly sweet sparklers to be better suited to morning consumption, making such Italian favorites as Asti, from the Piedmont, or Prosecco, from northeastern Italy, ideal choices.

BUONGIORNO!

1

BEVERAGES

Wherever you take your morning meal, and whatever its style, drinks are usually offered and served before a single bite of food is considered. Beverages are a great opportunity to start off a breakfast or brunch with the best of impressions, whether it's Italian-style coffee, a glass of sparkling blood-orange juice, or a more sophisticated cocktail that evokes a sunny terrazzo in Rome, Venice, or Tuscany.

Espresso

Le Ricette

Espresso—A Brewing Guide

There are so many different kinds of Italian and Italian-style espresso machines available to consumers for purchase today, many at surprisingly reasonable prices, that it would be presumptuous of me to provide precise brewing instructions. After all, each machine functions in its own unique way, and your best bet is to follow the manufacturer's operating instructions.

Nevertheless, when brewing espresso a few key principles apply regardless of the machine you use. Keep these brewing tips in mind whenever you make espresso or one of the classic espresso-based drink recipes that follow:

- Use a good espresso-style blend of coffees that have been roasted dark and mixed for a rich, complex flavor. Many popular purveyors of freshly roasted coffee offer "espresso" or "Italian" blends. Look also in Italian delis for vacuum-packed cans of whole-bean espresso imported from Italy.

- Starting with whole-bean coffee is important, because flavor dissipates quickly the moment coffee beans are ground. For that reason, grind your coffee just before brewing it. The proper grind for espresso is very fine and powdery. A burr-type coffee grinder, which pulverizes the beans rather than chopping them with whirring metal blades, is the best type of grinder for espresso, because it lets you set precisely the desired grind.

- Use a good-quality espresso machine that forces almost-boiling hot water at high pressure through the coffee. The old-fashioned two-part stovetop espresso pots, despite their charm, are difficult to use and simply don't deliver the same creamy intensity.
- Measure 1½ tablespoons of finely ground coffee for a single shot of espresso, twice that for a double shot. Tamp it down lightly but firmly in the machine's filter insert.
- Using whatever mechanism is used in your espresso machine, pass the heated water through the filter to brew the coffee. Use 1 ounce for a single shot and 2 ounces for a double shot. Turn off the machine as soon as the desired amount has been brewed.
- To steam milk with an espresso machine, fill a heatproof pitcher with cold whole, low-fat, or nonfat milk. Clip a cooking thermometer to the side of the pitcher, inside the milk. Insert the machine's steam nozzle deep into the milk. Open the valve, following the manufacturer's instructions. Heat the milk to 150–170°F on the thermometer. To build up a head of foam, position the pitcher so the nozzle's tip is just below the surface.

Cappuccino

This classic morning espresso drink is named for the Capuchin order of monks, since the cup of coffee is thought to resemble a brown-robed monk with a froth of white hair.

MAKES 1 SERVING

1 shot (1 ounce) freshly brewed espresso

Steamed and foamed milk

Cocoa powder or ground cinnamon (optional)

Sugar (optional)

Brew the espresso and pour it into a heated coffee cup. Pour in steamed milk to fill the cup about halfway. With a spoon, fill the rest of the cup with foam from the milk. Lightly sprinkle the foam with cocoa powder or ground cinnamon if you like. Add sugar to taste if desired.

ERSATZ ESPRESSO DRINKS

If you find yourself without an espresso machine, it is still possible to make coffee and coffee drinks that taste almost as good, using a drip filter. Start with good-quality espresso-roast coffee, freshly ground for the drip filter. Use one and a half to two times as much coffee as you would normally use—that is, 3 to 4 table-spoons of ground coffee for every 6 ounces of water, instead of 2 tablespoons. This will produce drip coffee with the strength and some of the flavor of true espresso, although it will lack the espresso's creamy body.

To approximate steamed and foamed milk, I've had some success using a food processor fitted with the metal blade or a blender. While the coffee is brewing, heat 1 cup of milk in a saucepan over medium heat until bubbles begin to form around its edges. Pour the milk into the processor or blender and put the lid on. (Take care to stand well clear of the machine and check carefully that the lid is on securely, covering it with a kitchen towel.) Turn on the machine briefly, just until some froth builds up on the milk. Then pour the hot, frothed milk into the brewed coffee for cappuccino or caffe latte, scooping up foam as desired.

Caffe Latte

This milky espresso drink is favored by many people first thing in the morning.

MAKES 1 SERVING

1 shot (1 ounce) freshly brewed espresso

Steamed and foamed milk
Sugar (optional)

Brew the espresso and pour it into a heated coffee cup. Pour in steamed milk to fill the cup almost to its rim. With a spoon, add a thin layer of frothy milk foam. Add sugar to taste if desired.

Adriatic Mist

Campari, the Italian bright red aperitif bitters, adds a wonderful contrast of flavor and color to these frosty, very grown-up brunch drinks. Of course, if your guests aren't partial to Campari, admittedly an acquired taste, you can leave it out of their glasses.

MAKES 4 SERVINGS

1 cup good-quality lemon sorbet

1 cup good-quality orange sorbet

1 cup Asti, Prosecco, or other good-quality medium-dry sparkling wine, well chilled

¼ cup Campari

6 long curls lemon zest, cut from a whole lemon's skin using a swivel-bladed vegetable peeler

Chill four tall champagne flutes in the freezer for at least 1 hour or fill them with ice, then add water to the rims and leave to chill for a few minutes, emptying them just before preparing the drinks.

Just before serving, put the sorbets and sparkling wine in a blender. Run just until they are blended smoothly to a thick but pourable consistency.

Put the Campari in a small measuring cup with a pouring lip. Holding the blender jar in one hand and the measuring cup in the other, carefully pour one-fourth each of the drink and the Campari into each glass so that the Campari forms a red stream through the thick, paler mixture along the length of the glass. Garnish each glass with a lemon curl and serve immediately.

Buongiorno Bellini

The Bellini cocktail originated in 1948 at Harry's Bar in Venice, Italy. Its creator, Harry Cipriani, named it after the celebrated fifteenth-century Venetian artist Jacopo Bellini, the drink reminiscent of his luminous paintings.

While you could go to the fuss of pureeing and sweetening fresh peaches, the widespread availability of good-quality bottled or canned peach nectar makes it far easier to make Bellini in a matter of moments. Seek out a good-quality medium-dry sparkling wine, whether Italian varieties such as Asti or Prosecco or another favorite.

MAKES 4 SERVINGS

1 cup good-quality peach nectar, well chilled

1 teaspoon fresh lemon juice

2 cups Asti, Prosecco, or other good-quality medium-dry sparkling wine, well chilled

4 small fresh mint sprigs

Chill four champagne flutes in the freezer for 1 hour or fill them with ice, then add water to the rims and leave to chill for a few minutes, emptying them just before preparing the drinks.

Into each of the chilled flutes, pour ¼ cup of the peach nectar and ¼ teaspoon of the lemon juice. Carefully pour the sparkling wine into each glass. With a swizzle stick or a long, slender spoon, gently stir each drink. Add a mint sprig to each glass and serve immediately.

Botticelli

I've taken the liberty of naming this sparkling raspberry cocktail after another famed Italian Renaissance painter. Tell your guests, if you like, that the color of the drink reminds you of the rosy flesh tones in his famous depiction of Venus. Make the drinks when fresh raspberries are at their summer peak or substitute defrosted frozen raspberries. Use a good Italian or other sparkling wine. Look for a good-quality raspberry liqueur or brandy.

You can make the berry puree ahead of time, mixing it with the liqueur and keeping it covered in the refrigerator as long as overnight.

MAKES 4 SERVINGS

1 cup fresh or defrosted frozen raspberries	2 cups Asti, Prosecco, or other good-quality medium-dry
½ cup raspberry liqueur	sparkling wine, well chilled

Chill four champagne flutes in the freezer for 1 hour or fill them with ice, then add water to the rims and leave to chill for a few minutes, emptying them just before preparing the drinks.

Reserve 1 dozen good whole raspberries. Put the rest in a blender or a food processor fitted with the metal blade and puree. Set a fine-meshed strainer over a bowl and pass the puree through the strainer to remove the seeds. Stir the raspberry liqueur into the puree.

Divide the puree-liqueur mixture evenly among the four chilled champagne flutes. Carefully pour the sparkling wine into each glass. With a swizzle stick or a long, slender spoon, gently stir each drink. Add 3 whole reserved berries to each glass and serve immediately.

Sparkling Blood-Orange Juice

The ruby color of blood oranges makes a startlingly beautiful juice, but the fruit can taste a bit tart for most people's liking. To that end, this recipe adds a virtually unnoticeable amount of sugar to make it taste as sweet as the orange juice most people enjoy. A splash of sparkling water makes it extra festive and refreshing for a special breakfast or brunch. Of course, you may replace the water with a sparkling wine of your choice.

MAKES 4 SERVINGS

18 blood oranges, cut in half

2 to 3 tablespoons sugar

1½ cups club soda or sparkling water

Using a citrus juicer, juice the oranges; you should have about 3 cups. Put the juice in a pitcher, taste a small sip, and add sugar to sweeten it to taste, stirring with a long-handled spoon until the sugar dissolves completely.

At serving time, pour the juice into wineglasses and add sparkling water.

Spumante Cocktail

My wife, Katie, and I have been partial to the classic champagne cocktail made with a bitters-soaked sugar cube ever since we first saw the movie Moonstruck. *This version is a particularly elegant way to start off a special-occasion Sunday brunch.*

Makes 4 servings

4 sugar cubes
2 very thin lemon slices, seeds
    removed, cut in half and
    twisted

Bottled bitters such as Angostura or
    Peychaud's
1 bottle Asti, Prosecco, or other
    good-quality medium-dry
    sparkling wine, well chilled

Chill four champagne flutes in the freezer for 1 hour or fill them with ice, then add water to the rims and leave to chill for a few minutes, emptying them just before preparing the drinks.

Shortly before serving, place the sugar cubes on an attractive plate. Place the twisted lemon slices on another plate. Present both plates at the table, or on a tray, accompanied by the chilled champagne flutes and the bottles of bitters and sparkling wine.

To serve, carefully drop 3 drops of bitters onto each sugar cube. Pour the sparkling wine into the flutes and ceremoniously drop 1 bitters-soaked sugar cube into each glass. Add a lemon slice to each glass and serve immediately.

Italian Hot Chocolate

Using imported semisweet European chocolate, such as Perugina (from Italy), Valrhona, Tobler, or Callebaut, melted in hot milk produces a steaming cup of superior quality. A splash of hazelnut-flavored Frangelico liqueur adds a touch of sophistication for the grown-ups.

MAKES 4 SERVINGS

¼ pound European semisweet
    chocolate, broken into small
    pieces or coarsely chopped

1 quart whole or low-fat milk
¾ cup Frangelico (optional)

Put the chocolate and milk in a saucepan. Warm over medium heat, stirring occasionally, until the milk gives off steam, about 5 minutes. With a wire whisk, stir briskly over the heat until the chocolate has melted completely and blended with the milk.

Ladle the hot chocolate into individual heated mugs. Pour 3 tablespoons of Frangelico into the mug of anyone who wants it and stir briefly to combine.

Mochaccino Smoothie

This simple blender recipe replicates the kind of iced coffee drinks so popular nowadays. It's perfect to offer at brunch on a hot summer day. You'll find chocolate sorbet in well-stocked supermarkets and specialty foods stores; I'm partial to the one from Häagen-Dazs.

MAKES 4 SERVINGS

3 cups extra-strong freshly brewed Italian-roast coffee, cooled to room temperature

3 cups good-quality chocolate sorbet

2 cups nonfat milk

¼ cup small semisweet chocolate chips

Whipped cream (optional)

Chill four tall 2-cup glasses in the freezer for at least 1 hour or fill them with ice cubes, then add water to the rims and leave to chill for a few minutes, emptying them just before preparing the drinks.

Put the coffee, sorbet, and milk in a blender. Process until blended smoothly. Pour into the chilled glasses and top with the chocolate chips and a dollop of whipped cream if desired. Serve with wide straws and long spoons.

2

EGG DISHES

For many Americans, eggs remain the defin-
itive breakfast ingredient. As demonstrated
by the following recipes, as well as the egg-
enriched morning pastas in Chapter 4, they can
star on the Italian-style morning table as well—
from scrambled eggs embellished with favorite
Mediterranean ingredients, to folded omelets
and the flat omelets called *frittatas*, to egg-
enriched baked dishes such as Italian-
inspired quiches and the savory or
sweet bread puddings known
as *stratas.*

Bacon and Tomato Scramble

Le Ricette

Bacon and Tomato Scramble *24*

Margherita Scramble *25*

Potato, Onion, and Fontina Scramble *26*

Fluffy Ricotta and Fresh Herb Scramble *27*

Creamy Parmesan Scramble *28*

Fonduta-Style Scramble with White Truffle Oil and Fontina *29*

Baked Eggs Florentine *31*

Baked Eggs Napoletano *33*

Eggs Beneditto with Parmesan-Pepper Beaten Biscuits,
Pancetta Pinwheels, and Blood-Orange Hollandaise *35*

Artichoke and Black Olive Frittata *37*

Green and Golden Squash, Ricotta, and Mint Frittata *39*

Roasted Red Pepper and Garlic Frittata *41*

Italian Herb Omelet *42*

Asparagus and Parmesan Omelet *44*

Mozzarella and Pesto Omelet *45*

Italian Sausage Omelet with Tomato Sauce *46*

Quiche Primavera *47*

Gorgonzola and Mushroom Quiche *49*

Pancetta and Sweet Onion Quiche *51*

Prosciutto, Sun-Dried Tomato, and Goat Cheese Quiche *53*

Three-Cheese and Sun-Dried Tomato Strata *55*

Provolone and Ham Strata *58*

Sweet Spiced Ricotta and Panettone Strata *59*

SCRAMBLES

Scrambled eggs mixed with complementary ingredients are among the quickest, easiest breakfast and brunch dishes to assemble and always deliver impressive results for the little time involved. The following recipes are at their best served freshly cooked. If you must hold them in a chafing dish or on a hot plate, keep them on the very soft and creamy side and cover the dish.

Bacon and Tomato Scramble

Rustic and simple, this scramble complements the smoky flavor of bacon with the sweetness of fresh tomato.

MAKES 4 TO 6 SERVINGS

4 Roma (plum) tomatoes
6 strips good-quality lean smoked
    bacon, cut crosswise into
    ½-inch pieces
3 tablespoons unsalted butter
2 shallots, minced

12 extra-large eggs, beaten until
    slightly frothy
Salt
Freshly ground black pepper
2 tablespoons finely shredded
    fresh basil

With the tip of a small, sharp knife, cut out the cores of the tomatoes. Cut each tomato in half crosswise and, with a fingertip, scoop out and discard the seeds. Cut the tomatoes into rough ½-inch dice.

Scatter the bacon pieces evenly in a nonstick skillet and cook over medium-low heat until golden brown, about 5 minutes. With a slotted spoon, remove the bacon from the pan and drain on paper towels. Pour off almost all of the fat from the skillet, leaving just a thin glistening.

Return the skillet to medium-low heat and add the butter and shallots. Sauté until the butter has melted and the shallots begin to sizzle, about 2 minutes. Add the eggs and cook, stirring continuously with a wooden spoon and scraping the bottom of the skillet, until the eggs form very moist, creamy curds. Stir in the tomato and bacon pieces, season to taste with salt and pepper, and continue cooking to your liking, taking care that the eggs remain on the soft and creamy side. Serve garnished with the basil.

Margherita Scramble

The flavor combination of a classic pizza topping finds new expression in this scramble. For the best texture and flavor, try to use fresh mozzarella, well drained, although the firmer packaged type will work well, too.

MAKES 4 TO 6 SERVINGS

3 tablespoons unsalted butter

12 oil-packed sun-dried tomato
    pieces, drained well and cut
    crosswise into ¼-inch-wide
    strips

12 extra-large eggs, beaten until
    slightly frothy

6 ounces mozzarella cheese, cut
    into ½-inch cubes (about
    1½ cups)

Salt

Freshly ground black pepper

3 tablespoons finely shredded
    fresh basil

Melt the butter in a skillet over medium-low heat. Add the sun-dried tomato pieces and sauté for about 1 minute.

Add the eggs and cook, stirring continuously with a wooden spoon and scraping the bottom of the skillet. The moment they begin to form curds but are still fairly liquid, stir in the mozzarella cubes. Continue cooking until the eggs form soft, creamy curds done to your liking but still moist. Season to taste with salt and pepper and stir in the basil.

Potato, Onion, and Fontina Scramble

This hearty, satisfying scramble is ideal to serve with thick slices of toasted sourdough on a brisk weekend morning. To speed things up, you could cook the potatoes the night before, dicing them just before you make the scramble.

MAKES 4 TO 6 SERVINGS

8 small red-skinned potatoes

2 tablespoons extra-virgin olive oil

2 tablespoons unsalted butter

1 small yellow onion, thinly sliced

12 extra-large eggs, beaten until
slightly frothy

¼ pound fontina cheese, shredded
(about 1 cup)

Salt

Freshly ground black pepper

1 tablespoon finely chopped fresh
Italian parsley

Put the potatoes in a saucepan and add lightly salted cold water to cover. Bring the water to a boil over high heat, reduce the heat to maintain a steady boil, and cook the potatoes until the tip of a small, sharp knife pierces them easily, about 15 minutes. Drain the potatoes well and, when they are cool enough to handle, cut them, skins and all, into ½-inch dice.

Put the oil and butter in a nonstick skillet over medium-low heat. When the butter has melted, add the potatoes and onion and cook until both vegetables begin to turn light golden, 7 to 10 minutes.

Add the eggs to the skillet and cook, stirring continuously with a wooden spoon and scraping the bottom of the skillet, until the eggs form very moist, creamy curds. Stir in the shredded fontina cheese, season to taste with salt and pepper, and continue cooking to your liking, taking care that the eggs remain on the soft and creamy side. Serve garnished with the parsley.

Fluffy Ricotta and Fresh Herb Scramble

Adding ricotta cheese to scrambled eggs gives them a delightfully light and fluffy consistency. Be sure to drain any liquid from the carton of ricotta.

MAKES 4 TO 6 SERVINGS

3 tablespoons unsalted butter

12 extra-large eggs, beaten until slightly frothy

6 tablespoons low-fat ricotta cheese

3 tablespoons freshly grated Parmesan cheese

2 tablespoons finely shredded fresh basil

2 tablespoons finely chopped fresh chives

2 tablespoons finely chopped fresh Italian parsley

Salt

Freshly ground white pepper

Melt the butter in a large skillet over medium-low heat. Add the eggs and cook, stirring continuously with a wooden spoon and scraping the bottom of the skillet, until the eggs begin to form curds but are still fairly liquid. Stir in the ricotta, Parmesan, basil, chives, and parsley. Continue cooking until the eggs form soft, creamy curds to your liking, seasoning to taste with salt and white pepper.

Creamy Parmesan Scramble

No morning egg dish could be simpler or more undeniably Italian in its appeal than this dish of scrambled eggs enriched with good-quality freshly grated Parmesan cheese. (Be sure, by the way, that the Parmesan is grated into fine particles rather than shredded.) For the best consistency, take care to keep the heat low and to stir the eggs continuously. Serve with any of the bruschettas in Chapter 5 or with sourdough toast and offer grilled ham, Griddled Prosciutto (see Index), or fresh sausages alongside.

Makes 4 to 6 servings

4 tablespoons unsalted butter, cut into small cubes

12 extra-large eggs, well beaten

¼ cup heavy cream or mascarpone

½ cup freshly grated Parmesan cheese

1 tablespoon finely shredded fresh basil

1 tablespoon finely chopped fresh chives

Freshly ground black pepper

Melt the butter in a heavy nonstick saucepan over very low heat. Add the eggs and cook, stirring and scraping continuously, until the eggs begin to thicken and form small, soft, very moist curds, 4 to 5 minutes.

Add the cream or mascarpone and sprinkle in the Parmesan. Continue stirring until the cheeses have melted and the eggs have cooked to a thick, fluffy, but still moist consistency, 3 to 4 minutes more.

Spoon the eggs onto heated plates and garnish with the basil and chives. Pass a pepper mill for guests to add freshly ground black pepper to taste.

Fonduta-Style Scramble with White Truffle Oil and Fontina

A specialty of the Piedmont in northwestern Italy, fonduta is the country's answer to cheese fondue, using fontina cheese in place of the traditional Swiss varieties. But it is also akin to elegant scrambled eggs, thickened as it usually is with egg yolks. The traditional crowning touch is shaved white truffles. For that rare and expensive extravagance, in this recipe I have substituted white truffle oil, which you can find in small bottles in gourmet markets, specialty foods stores, and some Italian delicatessens. Although still costly, a little of it goes a long way, and you can save the rest to toss with hot pasta, drizzle over sautéed or grilled veal, or use again to make these luscious eggs. Serve them with good toasted bread.

And, by the way, if you do come across a fresh white truffle in a gourmet market or Italian deli, omit the truffle oil from the recipe. Instead, shave the truffle tissue-thin over the eggs after you have spooned them onto the serving plates.

MAKES 4 TO 6 SERVINGS

3 tablespoons unsalted butter, cut into small cubes

12 extra-large eggs, well beaten

6 ounces fontina cheese, shredded (about 1½ cups)

1 tablespoon white truffle–flavored olive oil

2 tablespoons finely chopped fresh chives

Freshly ground black pepper

Salt

Melt the butter in a heavy nonstick saucepan over very low heat. Add the eggs and fontina and cook, stirring and scraping continuously with a wooden spoon, until they achieve a very thick, almost custardlike consistency, 7 to 10 minutes. Stir in the white truffle oil.

Spoon the eggs onto heated plates and garnish with chives. Pass a pepper mill and salt for guests to add to taste.

BAKED EGGS

Baked egg dishes, exemplified by the recipes that follow for Baked Eggs Florentine and Baked Eggs Napoletano, make a most impressive presentation for a special-occasion brunch. Though the recipes are longer than some, and may seem elaborate, they offer a busy cook the ease of advance preparation up to the point of the final baking. When guests arrive, all you have to do is take the dish out of the refrigerator and pop it into a preheated oven.

Baked Eggs Florentine

The base of creamed spinach in this pretty dish wins it the Florentine appellation—a preparation in the style of Florence, Italy. If you feel so inclined, sauté 1 to 2 ounces of thinly sliced, finely chopped pancetta along with the shallot or onion. Look in the market for bags of prewashed baby spinach leaves. If convenient, you can prepare the creamed spinach up to a day ahead, keeping it covered and refrigerated in a nonreactive bowl.

MAKES 6 TO 12 SERVINGS

2 tablespoons unsalted butter, plus
    extra for greasing
3 pounds baby spinach leaves
2 shallots or ½ small sweet onion,
    minced
1¼ cups heavy cream

¾ cup freshly grated Parmesan
    cheese
Pinch of freshly grated nutmeg
12 extra-large eggs
Freshly ground black pepper

Preheat the oven to 325°F. With some butter, generously grease a glass or porcelain baking dish about 6 to 8 inches wide, 12 inches long, and 1½ to 2 inches deep; alternatively, grease smaller individual-serving-sized baking dishes or ramekins. Bring a kettle of water to a boil.

    Rinse the spinach leaves with cold water until they are absolutely free of any grit; even if they've been prewashed, rinse them briefly so they'll have a little water clinging to their leaves. Put the spinach leaves with the water clinging to them in a large saucepan over medium heat; cover and cook for 5 minutes, tossing the pan occasionally. Empty the pan into a colander in the sink, rinse briefly with cold running water, and press down firmly on the spinach to squeeze out as much moisture as possible. Transfer the spinach to a cutting board and chop it coarsely.

Melt the 2 tablespoons butter in a large skillet over medium heat. Add the shallot or onion and sauté until lightly browned, 4 to 5 minutes. Add the cream, raise the heat to high, and bring it to a boil. Add the spinach and sprinkle in the Parmesan and the nutmeg. Cook, stirring, until the mixture is thick but still very moist, 2 to 3 minutes.

Spread the creamed spinach evenly in the prepared baking dish or dishes. Use the back of a large spoon to make 12 evenly spaced depressions in the spinach. Break 1 egg into each depression, taking care to keep the yolks whole.

Place the baking dish or dishes inside a roasting pan. Open the preheated oven, pull out the rack, and place the pan on top of it. Carefully pour the boiling water from the kettle into the pan to come halfway up the sides of the baking dish or dishes. Carefully slide the rack into the oven and bake until the egg whites are firm and opaque, about 25 minutes. To serve, use a large spoon to scoop each egg with its surrounding bed of spinach onto an individual plate, or place individual-serving baking dishes on top of large serving plates. Pass a pepper mill for guests to add freshly ground black pepper to taste.

Baked Eggs Napoletano

Tomato sauce is enhanced here with chunks of vegetable to form a robust foundation for baked eggs. The gentle baking further intensifies the sweet flavor of the tomatoes. If you like, make the chunky sauce up to a day ahead.

MAKES 6 TO 12 SERVINGS

¼ cup extra-virgin olive oil
2 green bell peppers, stemmed, seeded, and cut into ¾-inch dice
1 large onion, cut into ¾-inch chunks
1 cup pitted and halved black salt- or brine-cured Italian-style olives such as Gaeta, Liguria, or Lugano

Basic Tomato Sauce (see Index), made with canned diced tomatoes instead of crushed tomatoes
12 extra-large eggs
2 tablespoons finely shredded fresh basil leaves
2 tablespoons finely chopped fresh Italian parsley

Preheat the oven to 325°F. With 2 tablespoons of the olive oil, grease a glass or porcelain baking dish about 6 to 8 inches wide, 12 inches long, and 1½ to 2 inches deep; alternatively, grease smaller individual-serving-sized baking dishes or ramekins. Bring a kettle of water to a boil.

Heat the remaining 2 tablespoons olive oil in a large skillet over medium heat. Add the bell peppers and onion and sauté until they begin to wilt and color slightly, 4 to 5 minutes. Stir the sautéed vegetables and the black olives into the Basic Tomato Sauce.

Spread the sauce mixture evenly in the prepared baking dish or dishes. Use the back of a large spoon to make 12 evenly spaced depressions in the sauce. Break 1 egg into each depression, taking care to keep the yolks whole.

Place the baking dish or dishes inside a roasting pan. Open the preheated oven, pull out the rack, and place the pan on top of it. Carefully pour the boiling water from the kettle into the pan to come halfway up the sides of the baking dish or dishes. Carefully slide the rack into the oven and bake until the egg whites are firm and opaque, about 25 minutes. To serve, use a large spoon to scoop each egg with its surrounding bed of tomato sauce and vegetables onto an individual plate, or place individual-serving baking dishes on top of large serving plates. Garnish with basil and parsley.

Eggs Beneditto with Parmesan-Pepper Beaten Biscuits, Pancetta Pinwheels, and Blood-Orange Hollandaise

An emphatically Italian twist on the classic eggs Benedict, this impressive presentation is best reserved for a special-occasion brunch. Each element, however, is relatively easy to prepare. If you don't want to go to the trouble of baking Parmesan-Pepper Beaten Biscuits, by all means use good-quality split and toasted English muffins instead. If blood oranges are not available for the hollandaise, feel free to substitute regular orange juice or a 50-50 mixture of orange and lemon juices.

MAKES 6 SERVINGS

Blood-Orange Hollandaise

6 extra-large egg yolks

1 tablespoon grated blood-orange zest

2 tablespoons blood-orange juice

½ teaspoon salt

¼ teaspoon dry mustard

¼ teaspoon freshly ground white pepper

1½ cups (¾ pound) unsalted butter, cut into small pieces, at room temperature

12 Parmesan-Pepper Beaten Biscuits (see Index), cut with a 3-inch round cutter

12 slices Pancetta Pinwheels (see Index)

Eggs Beneditto

3 tablespoons extra-virgin olive oil

12 extra-large eggs

Salt

2 tablespoons finely shredded fresh basil leaves

First, make the hollandaise. In the bottom of a double boiler, bring 1 to 2 inches of water to a boil (the water level should not be high enough to touch the top pan). In the top of the double boiler, away from the heat, whisk together the egg yolks, blood-orange zest and juice, salt, mustard, and white pepper until smooth. Add about a third of the butter pieces. Reduce the heat under the double boiler to maintain a simmer and insert the top pan into the bottom. Stir continuously and briskly with a whisk until the ➤

butter melts and the sauce begins to thicken. While continuing to stir, add the remaining butter a few pieces at a time; keep stirring until all the butter has been added and the sauce thickens to a smooth, creamy, thick, but pourable consistency, 3 to 4 minutes more. Remove from the heat, cover, and keep warm. (If the sauce gets too thick, quickly whisk in 1 to 3 tablespoons hot water.)

While the biscuits are baking, cook the Pancetta Pinwheels. Keep them warm. (If you wish, you may make the biscuits ahead of time; warm them up just before serving.)

Just before serving, in one or two large nonstick skillets (you may use the same ones in which you cooked the pancetta, quickly wiping them with paper towels), heat the olive oil over medium-low heat. Break the eggs into the skillet(s) and sprinkle lightly with salt. Immediately cover the eggs with the skillets' lids or large pot lids and cook until the whites are set and light golden underneath and the yolks are beginning to thicken, 4 to 6 minutes.

To serve, place the warm biscuits on heated serving plates, two to a plate. Place a Pancetta Pinwheel on top of each biscuit and top with a fried egg. Drizzle the warm hollandaise sauce over the eggs, garnish with basil, and serve immediately.

FRITTATAS

In Italian kitchens, omelets are cooked as flat, thick pancakes called *frittatas*. A wide variety of fillings may be incorporated—vegetables, meats, cheeses—and the attractive result may be served hot or warm, cut into wedges.

The easiest way to cook a frittata, I have found, is to use a nonstick skillet with an ovenproof handle. The stick-resistant surface makes sure that the frittata stays whole and comes out of the pan easily. And starting it on the stovetop and finishing it in the oven ensures evenly cooked results.

Serve a frittata right out of the pan. Or invert a heatproof serving platter over the skillet, hold the skillet and platter together with pot holders, carefully invert them to unmold the frittata, and serve from the platter. If you like, accompany any of the following frittatas with Basic Tomato Sauce or Basic Pesto (see Index).

Artichoke and Black Olive Frittata

You can make this appealing frittata with either fresh artichokes or frozen artichoke hearts. The former will give you somewhat better flavor and texture, while the latter will cut down dramatically on the preparation time. Buy any flavorful variety of oil- or brine-cured black olives from an Italian deli or well-stocked supermarket.

MAKES 6 TO 8 SERVINGS

4 large fresh artichokes or 2
    9-ounce packages frozen
    artichoke hearts
½ lemon if using fresh artichokes
2 tablespoons extra-virgin olive oil
2 shallots, minced
10 extra-large eggs
¾ cup pitted and quartered cured
    black olives

¼ cup freshly grated Parmesan
    cheese
2 tablespoons finely shredded
    fresh basil leaves
2 tablespoons finely chopped fresh
    Italian parsley
2 tablespoons unsalted butter

Preheat the oven to 350°F.

If using fresh artichokes, fill a bowl with cold water and squeeze the lemon half into it to make acidulated water, which will prevent the artichokes from discoloring when they're trimmed. Starting at the base of each artichoke, pull off the leaves, stripping them downward toward the stem end and working around and around until you've removed all the leaves to above the artichoke's widest point. (Be careful: Some artichokes have leaves with sharp, spiny tips; if that is the case, wear kitchen gloves or snip off the tips with kitchen scissors first.) With a large, sharp knife, carefully cut off the remaining cone of leaves from the top third or so of each artichoke.

Then, starting at the base of each artichoke, use a small, sharp knife to carefully pare away the remaining dark-green outer skin. Dip the artichokes in the water. Then cut them into quarters and use the knife or a small, sharp-edged spoon to scoop out and discard the fuzzy chokes from the center of each quarter. Cut each quarter into thin slices.

If using frozen artichokes, defrost them and cut them into thin slices.

With paper towels, thoroughly pat dry the fresh or frozen artichoke slices. Heat the olive oil in a large skillet over high heat. Add the shallots and, as soon as they sizzle, add the artichoke slices. Sauté just until they begin to turn golden around the edges, 5 to 7 minutes. Transfer from the skillet to a clean bowl and leave until they are cool enough to touch.

In another bowl, beat the eggs until slightly frothy. Add the artichokes and shallots, olives, half of the Parmesan cheese, and the basil and parsley. Stir gently to combine the ingredients.

Melt the butter in a 10-inch nonstick ovenproof skillet over medium heat. Add the egg-artichoke mixture and press down with the back of a spoon or a spatula to smooth its surface. Sprinkle evenly with the remaining Parmesan. Reduce the heat to low and cook for about 2 minutes. Then transfer the skillet to the oven and bake until the frittata is fully set but still moist looking, about 20 minutes.

Serve the frittata hot from the oven or lukewarm, cut into wedges.

Green and Golden Squash, Ricotta, and Mint Frittata

Zucchini is a classic frittata filling. Here I've combined two different kinds of summer squash, along with a light, rich touch of ricotta and a refreshing hint of mint. If you wish, you can, of course, use zucchini on its own. Salting the zucchini at the beginning of the preparation eliminates much of the liquid from this moisture-laden vegetable.

MAKES 6 TO 8 SERVINGS

¾ pound small zucchini, trimmed

¾ pound yellow summer squash, trimmed

Salt

10 extra-large eggs

¼ pound part-skim-milk ricotta cheese, well drained

2 tablespoons freshly grated Parmesan cheese

2 tablespoons finely chopped fresh mint leaves

2 tablespoons unsalted butter

2 tablespoons extra-virgin olive oil

With the large holes of a box grater/shredder or the coarse shredding disk of a food processor, shred the zucchini and summer squash. Evenly spread a third of the shreds in a large colander set over a bowl or in the sink. Sprinkle evenly with salt, about 1 teaspoon in all. Spread another third of the shreds and sprinkle with 1 teaspoon more salt. Spread the remaining shreds and sprinkle with more salt. Leave to drain for 30 minutes to 1 hour. Then grab the shreds in small handfuls and squeeze firmly to eliminate every last bit of moisture; transfer each squeezed handful to a clean bowl. Discard all the juices. (Most of the salt will be eliminated with the juices.)

Preheat the oven to 350°F.

In another bowl, beat the eggs until slightly frothy. Add the squash shreds, ricotta, Parmesan, and mint. Stir gently to combine the ingredients, leaving the ricotta in tiny clumps.

Melt the butter with the olive oil in a 10-inch nonstick, ovenproof skillet over medium heat. Add the frittata mixture and press down with the back of a spoon or a spatula to smooth its surface. Reduce the heat to low and cook for about 2 minutes. Then transfer the skillet to the oven and bake until the frittata is fully set but still moist looking, about 20 minutes.

Serve the frittata hot from the oven or lukewarm, cut into wedges.

Roasted Red Pepper and Garlic Frittata

For the most colorful effect, look for bell peppers of varying colors—green, red, yellow, and orange. If you can't find a variety, I suggest sticking with red peppers, which will have the sweetest flavor. Draining the juices from the peppers will keep the frittata from getting too moist; reserve juices in the refrigerator to add to a salad dressing.

MAKES 6 TO 8 SERVINGS

1½ pounds bell peppers, roasted (see Index), stemmed and seeded, juices drained, and cut into ½-inch-wide strips

2 tablespoons extra-virgin olive oil

2 garlic cloves, minced

10 extra-large eggs

¼ cup freshly grated Parmesan cheese

2 tablespoons finely chopped fresh Italian parsley

2 tablespoons finely chopped fresh chives

2 tablespoons unsalted butter

Preheat the oven to 350°F.

Pat the bell peppers dry with paper towels. Heat the olive oil in a large skillet over medium heat. Add the garlic and, as soon as it sizzles, add the peppers. Sauté for about 3 minutes and transfer to a bowl to cool for about 5 minutes.

In another bowl, beat the eggs until slightly frothy. Add the pepper mixture, half of the Parmesan cheese, and the parsley and chives. Stir gently to combine the ingredients.

Melt the butter in a 10-inch nonstick ovenproof skillet over medium heat. Add the egg-pepper mixture and press down with the back of a spoon or a spatula to smooth its surface. Sprinkle evenly with the remaining Parmesan. Reduce the heat to low and cook for about 2 minutes. Then transfer the skillet to the oven and bake until the frittata is fully set but still moist looking, about 20 minutes.

Serve the frittata hot from the oven or lukewarm, cut into wedges.

FOLDED OMELETS

The classic folded omelet we normally associate with French cooking adapts well to Italian-style morning meals if you choose the right type of filling ingredients. It is best made to order, so each of the following recipes provides ingredients for just one serving.

If you like, have omelet making be the center-stage attraction of a brunch party. On the kitchen counter, set up an array of ready-to-use filling options from the following recipes. Have a bowl of whole eggs and bowls and forks for breaking and beating the eggs. Make sure you have a pair of good 8-inch nonstick omelet pans, the shallow kind with sloping sides, ready on each of your stove's two front burners. Demonstrate how to do it, then have your guests make their own, with two guests at a time working side by side.

Italian Herb Omelet

In France, one of the most classic of omelets is one filled simply with fines herbes, a mixture of fresh parsley, chives, chervil, and tarragon. Replacing them with popular Italian herbs gives this omelet a pleasing Mediterranean spin. Serve with some sliced prosciutto or Pancetta Pinwheels (see Index).

MAKES 1 SERVING

3 extra-large eggs
¼ teaspoon salt
Pinch of freshly ground white
    pepper
1 tablespoon unsalted butter
1 teaspoon finely shredded
    fresh basil

1 teaspoon finely chopped
    fresh chives
1 teaspoon finely chopped fresh
    Italian parsley
Fresh parsley sprig or basil leaf for
    garnish

In a small bowl, use a fork or wire whisk to beat the eggs, salt, and white pepper together until the eggs are slightly frothy.

Melt the butter in an 8-inch nonstick omelet pan over medium heat. Add the eggs. As they start to set, use a fork or a spatula to gently lift the edges and push them toward the center while you tilt the pan slightly to let the uncooked egg flow underneath.

Continue cooking until the eggs are almost completely set but still moist on top, 3 to 4 minutes. Sprinkle the top of the eggs evenly with the basil, chives, and parsley.

Shake the pan to see if the omelet slips easily in it; if not, carefully use the fork or spatula to loosen the edges. Lift the pan, hold the edge over a heated serving plate, and tilt the pan, shaking it gently, to start sliding the omelet out onto the plate. When the omelet is halfway out, twist your wrist to flip the pan over, folding the omelet in half. Garnish with a parsley sprig or basil leaf and serve immediately.

Asparagus and Parmesan Omelet

When fresh asparagus is in season, this simple omelet is sensational. Add some slivered prosciutto to the filling if you wish. Leaving the asparagus spears whole, with the tips poking out of the folded omelet's side, makes a very attractive presentation, though it requires more knife-and-fork work in the eating. Alternatively, cut the asparagus into pieces ranging in size from 1-inch to ¼-inch slices before precooking it.

MAKES 1 SERVING

3 asparagus spears, tough ends trimmed	1 tablespoon unsalted butter
3 extra-large eggs	3 tablespoons freshly grated Parmesan cheese
¼ teaspoon salt	Freshly ground black pepper

Lay the asparagus flat in a microwave-safe dish, add a splash of water, cover, and cook in the microwave until tender-crisp, following the manufacturer's suggested cooking times. Alternatively, bring 1 inch of water to a boil in a skillet wide enough to hold the asparagus flat; add the asparagus and boil until tender-crisp, about 3 minutes. Drain the asparagus and set aside.

In a small bowl, use a fork or wire whisk to beat the eggs and salt together until the eggs are slightly frothy.

Melt the butter in an 8-inch nonstick omelet pan over medium heat. Add the eggs. As they start to set, use a fork or a spatula to gently lift the edges and push them toward the center while you tilt the pan slightly to let the uncooked egg flow underneath.

Continue cooking until the eggs are almost completely set but still moist on top, 3 to 4 minutes. Sprinkle the top of the eggs with the Parmesan and add a little freshly ground black pepper to taste. Drape the 3 asparagus spears across the half of the omelet's surface nearest you, pushing them gently down into the egg.

Shake the pan to see if the omelet slips easily in it; if not, carefully use the fork or spatula to loosen the edges. Lift the pan, hold the edge nearest the asparagus over a heated serving plate, and tilt the pan, shaking it gently, to start sliding the omelet out onto the plate. When the omelet is halfway out, twist your wrist to flip the pan over, folding the other half of the omelet over the asparagus. Serve immediately.

Mozzarella and Pesto Omelet

Just 1 tablespoon of pesto adds a burst of aromatic flavor to this omelet. The mild taste and pleasantly chewy texture of mozzarella provide nice contrasts to the pesto and eggs. If you like, use an extra dab of pesto or some shredded fresh basil to garnish the top of the folded omelet.

MAKES 1 SERVING

3 extra-large eggs

¼ teaspoon salt

Pinch of freshly ground white
    pepper

1 tablespoon unsalted butter

1 tablespoon Basic Pesto (see Index)
    or store-bought pesto

2 ounces mozzarella cheese,
    shredded (about ½ cup)

In a small bowl, use a fork or wire whisk to beat the eggs, salt, and white pepper together until the eggs are slightly frothy.

Melt the butter in an 8-inch nonstick omelet pan over medium heat. Add the eggs. As they start to set, use a fork or a spatula to gently lift the edges and push them toward the center while you tilt the pan slightly to let the uncooked egg flow underneath.

Continue cooking until the eggs are almost completely set but still moist on top, 3 to 4 minutes. With the back of a tablespoon, spread the pesto evenly across the half of the omelet's surface nearest you. Sprinkle the shredded mozzarella evenly on top of the pesto.

Shake the pan to see if the omelet slips easily in it; if not, carefully use the fork or spatula to loosen the edges. Lift the pan, hold the edge nearest the pesto and cheese over a heated serving plate, and tilt the pan, shaking it gently, to start sliding the omelet out onto the plate. When the omelet is halfway out, twist your wrist to flip the pan over, folding the other half of the omelet over the cheese and pesto. Serve immediately.

Italian Sausage Omelet with Tomato Sauce

Use spicy or sweet Italian sausage made from pork, turkey, or chicken, as you like. For a party, precooking the sausage shortly before guests arrive will streamline the procedure.

MAKES 1 SERVING

1 fresh Italian sausage (4 to 6 ounces)
3 extra-large eggs
¼ teaspoon salt
1 tablespoon unsalted butter
¼ cup Basic Tomato Sauce (see Index), warmed in the

microwave or in a small saucepan
1 teaspoon finely shredded fresh basil leaves or finely chopped fresh Italian parsley

With the tip of a small, sharp knife, slit the casing of the sausage. Peel it off and discard it. Crumble the sausage meat into an 8-inch nonstick omelet pan. Cook over medium heat, stirring continuously with a wooden spoon and breaking up the meat into bite-sized pieces, until the sausage is cooked through and beginning to brown, about 5 minutes. Transfer the sausage meat to a small bowl; discard the fat from the pan and clean out and dry the pan.

In a small bowl, use a fork or wire whisk to beat the eggs and salt together until the eggs are slightly frothy.

Melt the butter in the omelet pan over medium heat. Add the eggs. As they start to set, use a fork or a spatula to gently lift the edges and push them toward the center while you tilt the pan slightly to let the uncooked egg flow underneath.

Continue cooking until the eggs are almost completely set but still moist on top, 3 to 4 minutes. Scatter the cooked sausage pieces evenly over the half of the omelet's surface nearest you, pushing them gently down into the egg.

Shake the pan to see if the omelet slips easily in it; if not, carefully use the fork or spatula to loosen the edges. Lift the pan, hold the edge nearest the sausage over a heated serving plate, and tilt the pan, shaking it gently, to start sliding the omelet out onto the plate. When the omelet is halfway out, twist your wrist to flip the pan over, folding the other half of the omelet over the sausage. Spoon the heated tomato sauce over the omelet, garnish with basil or parsley, and serve immediately.

ITALIAN-STYLE QUICHES

Quiche is a classic French savory egg-filled tart, but it adapts itself well to Italian ingredients and seasonings for a breakfast or brunch main dish that is impressive and very satisfying yet quite easy to make. Use the Basic Tart Pastry recipe (see Index) for any of the quiches that follow. The quiche will be easier to bake and serve if you make it in a metal tart pan with a removable bottom, available in any well-stocked kitchenware store.

Serve the quiche hot from the oven if you like, especially on a cool morning. It is also excellent at room temperature.

Quiche Primavera

Primavera means "springtime" in Italian, but the widespread availability of good-quality fresh produce makes it possible to enjoy this quiche with its colorful bouquet of vegetables at any time of year. You may substitute any other firm-textured, nonwatery vegetables you like and that go together well. The fresh herbs and Parmesan cheese add just the right Italian touch.

MAKES 1 9-INCH QUICHE; 6 TO 8 SERVINGS

Basic Tart Pastry (see Index)
2 tablespoons unsalted butter
1 small yellow onion, cut into
    ¼-inch dice
1 red bell pepper, quartered,
    stemmed, seeded, and cut
    crosswise into ¼-inch-wide
    strips
½ cup small broccoli florets
½ cup thinly sliced fresh
    asparagus

3 extra-large eggs
1½ cups half-and-half
6 tablespoons freshly grated
    Parmesan cheese
2 tablespoons finely shredded
    fresh basil leaves
1 tablespoon finely chopped fresh
    Italian parsley
¼ teaspoon salt
¼ teaspoon freshly ground black
    pepper

Preheat the oven to 425°F.

On a lightly floured work surface, use a rolling pin to roll out the pastry dough into an even circle 12 inches in diameter. Loosely roll up the circle around the rolling pin, transfer it to a 9-inch tart pan with a removable bottom, and unroll. With your fingers, gently press the dough into the pan. Use a small, sharp knife to carefully trim the dough even with the edge of the pan.

With a fork, prick the dough's bottom and sides all over. Tear off a 24-inch-long sheet of aluminum foil, fold it in half, poke a few holes in it, and press it down inside the tart pan to cover the dough. Bake for 8 minutes, then remove the foil and continue baking until the pastry looks dry and firm but not yet brown, about 4 minutes more. Remove the pan from the oven. Reduce the oven temperature to 325°F.

Bring a large pan of water to a boil.

Meanwhile, melt the butter in a small skillet over medium heat. Add the onion and bell pepper and sauté until tender and the onion is just beginning to turn golden, 5 to 7 minutes.

When the water boils, add the broccoli florets and boil for about 3 minutes. Add the asparagus and boil for about 2 minutes more, until the vegetables are just beginning to be tender. Drain well, then transfer to a kitchen towel and pat dry.

In a mixing bowl, beat the eggs until slightly frothy. Stir in the half-and-half, Parmesan, basil, parsley, salt, and pepper.

Arrange the broccoli, asparagus, onion, and bell pepper pieces evenly inside the pastry shell. Pour the egg mixture evenly over the vegetables. Carefully transfer the filled quiche to the oven and bake until a knife inserted into the center comes out clean, 35 to 40 minutes. If the edges appear to be browning too quickly before the quiche is done, carefully cover them with strips of aluminum foil, placed shiny side out.

Transfer the quiche to a wire rack to cool on the kitchen counter for about 15 minutes. To unmold, place the quiche on top of a plate smaller than its bottom or on top of a wide can; then gently pull down its side, using a knife tip to loosen the edges of the pastry if necessary. Cut into wedges and serve.

Gorgonzola and Mushroom Quiche

The famed Italian blue-veined cheese lends eye-opening flavor and richness to this quiche. Sautéed mushrooms bring the assertive cheese back down to earth. Serve some fresh fruit on the side to counterbalance the strong flavors.

MAKES 1 9-INCH QUICHE; 6 TO 8 SERVINGS

Basic Tart Pastry (see Index)
2 tablespoons unsalted butter
2 shallots, minced
1 pound mushrooms, sliced ¼ inch thick
3 extra-large eggs
1½ cups milk

2 tablespoons finely shredded fresh basil leaves
¼ teaspoon salt
¼ teaspoon freshly ground black pepper
6 ounces Gorgonzola cheese

Preheat the oven to 425°F.

On a lightly floured work surface, use a rolling pin to roll out the pastry dough into an even circle 12 inches in diameter. Loosely roll up the circle around the rolling pin, transfer it to a 9-inch tart pan with a removable bottom, and unroll. With your fingers, gently press the dough into the pan. Use a small, sharp knife to carefully trim the dough even with the edge of the pan.

With a fork, prick the dough's bottom and sides all over. Tear off a 24-inch-long sheet of aluminum foil, fold it in half, poke a few holes in it, and press it down inside the tart pan to cover the dough. Bake for 8 minutes, then remove the foil and continue baking until the pastry looks dry and firm but not yet brown, about 4 minutes more. Remove the pan from the oven. Reduce the oven temperature to 325°F.

Melt the butter in a large skillet over medium heat. Add the shallots and sauté until they begin to get tender, 3 to 5 minutes. Add the mushrooms, raise the heat to medium-high, and continue sautéing, stirring frequently, until most of the liquid the mushrooms give up has evaporated and they begin to brown, 7 to 10 minutes.

In a mixing bowl, beat the eggs until slightly frothy. Stir in the milk, basil, salt, and pepper.

Spread the mushrooms evenly inside the pastry shell. Dot small clumps of the Gorgonzola evenly on top of the mushrooms. Pour in the egg mixture, covering the mushrooms and cheese. Carefully transfer the filled quiche to the oven and bake until a knife inserted into the center comes out clean, 35 to 40 minutes. If the edges appear to be browning too quickly before the quiche is done, carefully cover them with strips of aluminum foil, placed shiny side out.

Transfer the quiche to a wire rack to cool on the kitchen counter for about 15 minutes. To unmold, place the quiche on top of a plate smaller than its bottom or on top of a wide can; then gently pull down its side, using a knife tip to loosen the edges of the pastry if necessary. Cut into wedges and serve.

Pancetta and Sweet Onion Quiche

Think of this as an Italian-style tribute to the classic bacon-and-leek quiche Lorraine of France. For the desired sweet onion flavor, look for such popular varieties as Maui, Walla Walla, Vidalia, or Texas Sweet. Of course, you may substitute any other type of bacon you like if you can't lay your hands on pancetta.

MAKES 1 9-INCH QUICHE; 6 TO 8 SERVINGS

Basic Tart Pastry (see Index)
2 tablespoons unsalted butter
1 large sweet yellow onion, halved
    lengthwise and cut crosswise
    into ¼-inch slices
6 ounces thinly sliced pancetta, cut
    into ¼-inch-wide strips
3 extra-large eggs
1½ cups half-and-half
2 tablespoons finely shredded fresh
    basil leaves

1 tablespoon finely chopped
    fresh chives
¼ teaspoon salt
¼ teaspoon freshly ground black
    pepper
Pinch of freshly grated nutmeg
6 ounces provolone cheese,
    shredded (about 1½ cups)
1½ teaspoons cornstarch

Preheat the oven to 425°F.

On a lightly floured work surface, use a rolling pin to roll out the pastry dough into an even circle 12 inches in diameter. Loosely roll up the circle around the rolling pin, transfer it to a 9-inch tart pan with a removable bottom, and unroll. With your fingers, gently press the dough into the pan. Use a small, sharp knife to carefully trim the dough even with the edge of the pan.

With a fork, prick the dough's bottom and sides all over. Tear off a 24-inch-long sheet of aluminum foil, fold it in half, poke a few holes in it, and press it down inside the tart pan to cover the dough. Bake for 8 minutes, then remove the foil and continue baking until the pastry looks dry and firm but not yet brown, about 4 minutes more. Remove the pan from the oven. Reduce the oven temperature to 325°F.

Melt the butter in a large skillet over medium heat. Add the onion and sauté for about 7 minutes. Add the pancetta and continue sautéing until the onion begins to turn golden, 2 to 3 minutes more. Carefully pour off any excess fat from the skillet and set the mixture aside.

In a mixing bowl, beat the eggs until slightly frothy. Stir in the half-and-half, basil, chives, salt, pepper, and nutmeg. Put the shredded provolone in a separate bowl, sprinkle evenly with the cornstarch, and toss lightly to coat.

Stir the cheese and the onion-pancetta mixture into the egg mixture. Pour the egg mixture into the pastry shell, distributing the solids evenly. Carefully transfer the filled quiche to the oven and bake until a knife inserted into the center comes out clean, 35 to 40 minutes. If the edges appear to be browning too quickly before the quiche is done, carefully cover them with strips of aluminum foil, placed shiny side out.

Transfer the quiche to a wire rack to cool on the kitchen counter for about 15 minutes. To unmold, place the quiche on top of a plate smaller than its bottom or on top of a wide can; then gently pull down its side, using a knife tip to loosen the edges of the pastry if necessary. Cut into wedges and serve.

Prosciutto, Sun-Dried Tomato, and Goat Cheese Quiche

The intense yet pleasing flavors of this quiche's filling firmly root it in Italian cuisine.

MAKES 1 9-INCH QUICHE; 6 TO 8 SERVINGS

Basic Tart Pastry (see Index)

6 ounces fresh, creamy goat cheese

3 extra-large eggs

1½ cups half-and-half

2 tablespoons finely shredded fresh basil leaves

1 tablespoon finely chopped fresh chives

¼ teaspoon salt

¼ teaspoon freshly ground black pepper

¼ pound thinly sliced prosciutto, cut into ¼-inch-wide strips

12 oil-packed sun-dried tomato pieces, drained and cut into ¼-inch-wide strips

Preheat the oven to 425°F.

On a lightly floured work surface, use a rolling pin to roll out the pastry dough into an even circle 12 inches in diameter. Loosely roll up the circle around the rolling pin, transfer it to a 9-inch tart pan with a removable bottom, and unroll. With your fingers, gently press the dough into the pan. Use a small, sharp knife to carefully trim the dough even with the edge of the pan.

With a fork, prick the dough's bottom and sides all over. Tear off a 24-inch-long sheet of aluminum foil, fold it in half, poke a few holes in it, and press it down inside the tart pan to cover the dough. Bake for 8 minutes, then remove the foil and continue baking until the pastry looks dry and firm but not yet brown, about 4 minutes more. Remove the pan from the oven. Reduce the oven temperature to 325°F.

Put the goat cheese, eggs, and half-and-half in a food processor fitted with the metal blade. Pulse the machine several times until they are blended smoothly. Add the basil, chives, salt, and pepper and pulse two or three times more to combine.

Pour the cheese-egg mixture into the pastry shell. Scatter the prosciutto and sun-dried tomato pieces evenly over the surface and, with a fork, gently press them down into the cheese mixture to submerge them almost but not quite completely. Carefully transfer the filled quiche to the oven and bake until a knife inserted into the center comes out clean, 35 to 40 minutes. If the edges appear to be browning too quickly before the quiche is done, carefully cover them with strips of aluminum foil, placed shiny side out.

Transfer the quiche to a wire rack to cool on the kitchen counter for about 15 minutes. To unmold, place the quiche on top of a plate smaller than its bottom or on top of a wide can; then gently pull down its side, using a knife tip to loosen the edges of the pastry if necessary. Cut into wedges and serve.

STRATAS

The Italianate name describes the layers that make up this enhanced savory or sweet version of a bread pudding, a wonderfully homey dish to serve for breakfast or brunch accompanied by sausages or a fresh fruit salad.

Your success will depend in large part on selecting a good loaf of bread to use as the basis for the pudding. For savory versions, go to a good-quality bakery or well-stocked supermarket for a rustic Italian loaf with a fairly firm crumb. You'll find the panettone for the sweet version in Italian delis or specialty foods stores.

A strata makes a great dish for morning entertaining because you can assemble it as far in advance as a full day before. Cover and refrigerate the uncooked pudding. Then remove it, uncover, and put it in the oven before guests arrive.

Three-Cheese and Sun-Dried Tomato Strata

This version of a strata presents a classic combination of favorite Italian flavors.

MAKES 8 TO 12 SERVINGS

18 ½-inch-thick slices day-old good-quality rustic Italian or sourdough bread, crusts trimmed

2 cups milk

6 extra-large eggs, lightly beaten

1 cup half-and-half

½ pound mozzarella cheese, shredded (about 2 cups)

½ pound fontina cheese, shredded (about 2 cups)

1 cup freshly grated Parmesan cheese

1 cup oil-packed sun-dried tomatoes, drained well and cut into thin slivers

⅓ cup packed finely shredded fresh basil leaves

Preheat the oven to 350°F. Butter a 3-quart glass or porcelain baking dish measuring about 9 by 13 inches.

➤

Put the bread slices in a large bowl and pour the milk over them. Leave them to soak for about 15 minutes, turning them over once or twice.

In another bowl, stir together the eggs, half-and-half, mozzarella, fontina, and Parmesan.

Arrange one-third of the bread slices in the bottom of the baking dish. Scatter on a third each of the sun-dried tomatoes and the basil, then spread on one-third of the egg-cheese mixture. Repeat with two more layers each of the remaining bread, tomatoes and basil, and egg-cheese mixture.

Put the baking dish in the oven and bake, uncovered, until the strata is bubbly and golden brown, about 1 hour. Remove from the oven and let stand for about 10 minutes before scooping with a large metal serving spoon onto individual heated plates.

Provolone and Ham Strata

The appeal of a classic grilled sandwich is translated here into a savory strata. Use a good-quality smoked ham, thinly sliced.

Makes 8 to 12 servings

18 ½-inch-thick slices day-old
good-quality rustic Italian or
sourdough bread, crusts
trimmed

2 cups milk

6 extra-large eggs, lightly beaten

1 cup half-and-half

¾ pound provolone cheese,
shredded (about 3 cups)

¾ cup freshly grated Parmesan
cheese

¼ cup finely chopped fresh Italian
parsley

¼ cup finely chopped fresh chives

¾ pound smoked ham, thinly sliced

Preheat the oven to 350°F. Butter a 3-quart glass or porcelain baking dish measuring about 9 by 13 inches.

Put the bread slices in a large bowl and pour the milk over them. Leave them to soak for about 15 minutes, turning them over once or twice.

In another bowl, stir together the eggs, half-and-half, provolone, Parmesan, parsley, and chives.

Arrange one-third of the bread slices in the bottom of the baking dish. Drape a third of the ham on top, then spread on one-third of the egg-cheese mixture. Repeat with two more layers each of the remaining bread, ham, and egg-cheese mixture.

Put the baking dish in the oven and bake, uncovered, until the strata is bubbly and golden brown, about 1 hour. Remove from the oven and let stand for about 10 minutes before scooping with a large metal serving spoon onto individual heated plates.

Sweet Spiced Ricotta and Panettone Strata

The festive, fruit-laden bread known as panettone, *widely available in Italian markets and specialty foods stores, makes a delightful sweet version of a morning bread pudding. Offer Pancetta Pinwheels (see Index) or grilled sweet Italian sausages on the side.*

MAKES 8 TO 12 SERVINGS

¾ cup slivered almonds

18 ½-inch-thick slices panettone

2 cups milk

6 extra-large eggs, lightly beaten

1 cup half-and-half

1 pound part-skim-milk
  ricotta cheese

¾ cup golden raisins

¼ cup packed light brown sugar

2 teaspoons ground cinnamon

Pinch of freshly grated nutmeg

Preheat the oven to 350°F. Butter a 3-quart glass or porcelain baking dish measuring about 9 by 13 inches. Spread the almonds in a small baking dish and bake them in the oven until light golden in color, 5 to 7 minutes.

Put the panettone slices in a large bowl and pour the milk over them. Leave them to soak for about 15 minutes, turning them over once or twice.

In another bowl, stir together the eggs, half-and-half, ricotta, raisins, brown sugar, cinnamon, nutmeg, and toasted almonds.

Arrange one-third of the panettone slices in the bottom of the baking dish. Spread a third of the egg-cheese mixture over them. Repeat with two more layers each of the remaining bread and egg-cheese mixture.

Put the baking dish in the oven and bake, uncovered, until the strata is bubbly and golden brown, about 1 hour. Remove from the oven and let stand for about 10 minutes before scooping with a large metal serving spoon onto individual heated plates.

3

GRIDDLE
FAVORITES

Pancakes, waffles, and French toast bring a special feeling of
celebration to weekend breakfasts or brunches. The recipes that
follow show just how easy it can be to introduce Italian-style flair to such
dishes, from the ricotta that makes pancakes especially light and fluffy
to the basic crepelike crespelle that welcome so many elaborations,
from the toasted hazelnuts that enrich crisp and
creamy waffles to the French toast that
becomes extraordinary when you use
panettone in place of the more
usual kinds of bread.

Lemon Ricotta Pancakes with Quick Raspberry Compote

Le Ricette

Lemon Ricotta Pancakes with Quick Raspberry Compote

Adding ricotta cheese to basic pancake ingredients produces remarkably fluffy, rich griddle cakes that are enlivened here by the zest (the colorful outermost layer of peel) and juice of lemons. A quickly made compote of raspberries perfectly complements their flavor and color. If you don't like raspberry seeds, press the compote through a fine-meshed strainer to make a smooth raspberry sauce.

MAKES 24 PANCAKES; 4 TO 6 SERVINGS

1¼ cups all-purpose flour

⅓ cup sugar

2 teaspoons baking powder

½ teaspoon baking soda

¼ teaspoon salt

1 cup milk

1 cup ricotta cheese

3 tablespoons unsalted butter, melted

2 extra-large eggs, separated

2 tablespoons grated lemon zest

2 teaspoons fresh lemon juice

Quick Raspberry Compote

1 cup fresh raspberries

2 tablespoons unsalted butter

2 to 3 tablespoons sugar

1 teaspoon fresh lemon juice

Preheat the oven to 200°F.

In a mixing bowl, stir together the flour, sugar, baking powder, baking soda, and salt. In another bowl, whisk together the milk, ricotta, melted butter, egg yolks, lemon zest, and lemon juice. Add the ricotta mixture to the flour mixture and stir with a whisk just until combined.

Heat a large skillet or griddle over medium heat.

In another clean bowl, beat the egg whites with an electric mixer or wire whisk until they form stiff peaks when the beaters or whisk is lifted out. With a rubber spatula, gently fold the egg whites into the batter until only streaks of white remain.

Lightly spray the skillet or griddle with nonstick spray. Spoon the batter onto the griddle in heaping tablespoons to form circular cakes about 3 inches in diameter. Cook until each cake looks slightly dry around the edges and its underside is lightly browned, about 1 minute. Flip and cook until the other side is golden, about 1 minute more. Transfer to a baking dish, cover loosely with foil, and keep warm in the oven while preparing the rest of the batter.

When the final pancakes are cooking, make the raspberry compote. Reserving a few berries to garnish each serving, put the remaining berries and the butter, sugar, and lemon juice into a small saucepan. Cook over medium heat, stirring frequently, until the butter has melted, the sugar has dissolved, and the berries barely begin to soften and give up their juices, about 2 minutes.

To serve, arrange the pancakes slightly overlapping on heated individual serving plates. Spoon the berry compote on top, garnish with the reserved berries, and serve immediately.

Mochaccino Ricotta Pancakes

The fluffiness of the ricotta cheese in these griddle cakes perfectly suits the flavors of Italian coffee and semisweet chocolate. While true coffee fanatics would naturally shy away from instant espresso powder, it works surprisingly well as a flavoring. A generous mound of whipped cream (go ahead and use an aerosol can of the real dairy stuff if you must) evokes the frothy head of steamed milk on top of a classic cappuccino. For any guests whose sweet tooth might not be fully satisfied, have some warm syrup ready on the side.

MAKES 12 PANCAKES; 4 TO 6 SERVINGS

Whipped Cream
1 cup whipping cream
1½ tablespoons sugar
½ teaspoon pure vanilla extract

Pancakes
1¼ cups all-purpose flour
⅓ cup sugar
2 teaspoons baking powder
½ teaspoon baking soda
¼ teaspoon salt

1 cup milk
1 cup ricotta cheese
3 tablespoons unsalted butter, melted
2 extra-large eggs, separated
1 tablespoon instant espresso powder
2 teaspoons hot water
½ cup small semisweet chocolate chips
Ground cinnamon for garnish

Make the whipped cream at least 1 hour before serving. Put the cream, sugar, and vanilla in a chilled mixing bowl. With chilled beaters, use an electric mixer to beat the cream at medium speed until it forms soft peaks when the beaters are lifted out. Cover the bowl with plastic wrap and refrigerate.

Preheat the oven to 200°F.

In a mixing bowl, stir together the flour, sugar, baking powder, baking soda, and salt. In another bowl, whisk together the milk, ricotta, melted butter, and egg yolks. In a small cup, stir together the espresso powder and hot water until the powder dissolves, then stir it into the ricotta mixture. Add the ricotta mixture to the flour mixture and stir with a whisk just until combined.

Heat a large skillet or griddle over medium heat.

In another clean bowl, beat the egg whites with an electric mixer or wire whisk until they form stiff peaks when the beaters or whisk is lifted out. With a rubber spatula, gently fold the egg whites into the batter until only streaks of white remain.

Lightly spray the skillet or griddle with nonstick spray. Spoon the batter onto the griddle 2 heaping tablespoons at a time, forming circular cakes about 6 inches in diameter. Immediately scatter about 2 teaspoons of chocolate chips evenly over each cake. Cook until the cakes look slightly dry around the edges and their undersides are lightly browned, about 1 minute. Flip and cook until the other sides are golden, about 1 minute more. Transfer to a baking dish, cover loosely with foil, and keep warm in the oven while preparing the rest of the batter.

To serve, stack the pancakes neatly on individual heated serving plates. Generously mound the chilled whipped cream on top and dust with cinnamon. Serve immediately.

Polenta Blueberry Pancakes

These tender pancakes highlight Italy's famous cornmeal, contrasting its vibrant hue and earthy flavor with the deep blue color and sweet flavor of the berries. Because the pancakes cook so quickly, instant polenta works best for this recipe. If fresh blueberries aren't in season, or you're not partial to the berries, just leave them out.

MAKES ABOUT 12 PANCAKES; 4 TO 6 SERVINGS

⅔ cup instant polenta	2 extra-large eggs, lightly beaten
⅔ cup all-purpose flour	1 cup milk
2 teaspoons sugar	¾ cup unsalted butter, melted
1½ teaspoons baking powder	¾ cup maple or pancake syrup
½ teaspoon salt	1 cup fresh blueberries

Preheat the oven to 200°F.

In a mixing bowl, stir together the polenta, flour, sugar, baking powder, and salt. In a separate bowl, stir together the eggs, milk, and ¼ cup of the melted butter.

Keep the remaining butter warm. Put the syrup in a small saucepan and warm it over very low heat while you cook the pancakes.

Add the liquid ingredients to the dry ingredients and stir with a whisk just until combined. Heat a large skillet or griddle over medium heat.

Spray the skillet or griddle with nonstick spray. Spoon the batter onto the pan or griddle 2 tablespoons at a time to form pancakes about 4 inches in diameter. As soon as each pancake is formed, scatter a scant tablespoon of blueberries across its surface. Cook until the pancakes look slightly dry around the edges, their surfaces are covered with bubbles, and their undersides are golden brown, 1 to 2 minutes. Flip and cook until the other sides are golden brown, 1 to 2 minutes more. Transfer to a baking dish, cover loosely with foil, and keep warm in the oven while preparing the rest of the batter, stirring the batter before spooning each batch.

To serve, stack the pancakes or arrange them slightly overlapping on individual heated serving plates. Pass the remaining melted butter and the warm syrup for guests to add to taste.

Panettone French Toast with Caramelized Apples

Panettone, the column-shaped Italian festival bread, makes wonderful French toast. Here the French toast is topped with quickly sautéed apples; but you could, instead, serve it simply with syrup or jam or topped with lightly sugared sliced ripe strawberries. Although the slices will be slender wedges, aim to cut them the approximate size of standard bread loaf slices. If you can't find panettone, substitute egg bread or challah.

MAKES 4 SERVINGS

¼ cup slivered almonds

Caramelized Apples
2 tablespoons unsalted butter
2 Golden Delicious or Granny Smith
    apples, peeled, cored, and cut
    into ½-inch-thick wedges
¼ cup apple juice
3 tablespoons honey
Pinch of freshly grated nutmeg

Panettone French Toast
2 extra-large eggs, lightly
    beaten
½ cup low-fat milk
1 tablespoon sugar
½ teaspoon almond extract
8 ¾-inch-thick slices panettone
    or egg bread
4 tablespoons unsalted butter

Preheat the oven to 325°F. Put the almonds in a baking dish and toast in the oven until golden, 5 to 7 minutes. Reduce the oven temperature to 200°F.

For the caramelized apples, melt the butter in a nonstick skillet over medium heat. Add the apples and sauté until lightly browned, about 5 minutes. Add the apple juice, honey, and nutmeg and continue cooking, stirring frequently, until the apples are tender and a thick, caramel-like sauce has formed. Cover and keep warm.

To make the French toast, stir together the eggs, milk, sugar, and almond extract in a wide, shallow bowl or baking dish. Add the bread slices to the mixture, turning to coat them evenly on both sides and then leaving them to soak.

Meanwhile, melt half of the butter in another nonstick skillet over medium heat. Add half of the bread slices and cook them until golden brown, 4 to 5 minutes per side. Transfer them to a baking dish, cover with aluminum foil, and put in the oven to keep warm. Melt the remaining butter in the skillet and cook the remaining French toast. Serve topped with the caramelized apples and garnished with the toasted almonds.

Crespelle with Orange Marmalade Sauce

Crespelle are the crepes of Italy, thin, delicate pancakes that you can enjoy on their own, as in this recipe, or fill, shape, and serve in a number of imaginative ways, as the recipes that follow demonstrate. Making the batter in advance ensures more tender results as well as cutting down on your work before serving time.

MAKES ABOUT 24 CRESPELLE; 6 TO 8 SERVINGS

Basic Crespelle
1¼ cups all-purpose flour
1 cup milk
½ cup water
2 tablespoons sugar
¼ teaspoon salt
4 extra-large eggs

4 tablespoons unsalted butter

Orange Marmalade Sauce
½ cup (¼ pound) unsalted butter
½ cup thin-shred orange
   marmalade
½ cup light corn syrup

To make the batter, put the flour, milk, water, sugar, salt, and eggs in a blender or a food processor fitted with the metal blade. Process until well blended, about 1 minute, stopping once or twice to scrape down the bowl. Transfer to a mixing bowl, cover, and refrigerate for at least 1 hour or as long as overnight.

In a nonstick crepe pan or another 6- to 7-inch skillet with shallow sides, melt the 4 tablespoons butter. Pour it into a small bowl and put the butter-coated pan aside. Leave the butter to cool for 5 minutes. With a wire whisk, stir the butter into the batter.

Return the butter-coated pan to medium-high heat. With a tablespoon, spoon 2 tablespoons of the batter into the hot pan, gently spreading the batter with the back of the spoon to coat the pan evenly. Cook until the surface begins to look dry and the underside is golden brown, about 30 seconds. Loosen the edges with a thin spatula and flip the crespelle, cooking the other side until it begins to brown, about 30 seconds more. Repeat with the remaining batter, stacking the crespelle between squares of wax paper and keeping them covered and warm with a sheet of aluminum foil.

When all the crespelle are done, make the sauce by putting the ½ cup butter with the marmalade and the corn syrup in a small saucepan over low heat. Stir until the butter and marmalade have melted. Arrange the crespelle, folded if you like, overlapping on heated serving plates and spoon the butter-marmalade mixture over them.

Baked Ricotta-Filled Crespelle with Marsala-Soaked Raisins

You might think of these as Italian-style blintzes. Present them in a pretty oven-to-table baking dish.

MAKES ABOUT 24 CRESPELLE; 6 TO 8 SERVINGS

Basic Crespelle (see Index)
1 cup marsala
1 cup golden raisins
6 tablespoons unsalted butter
2 cups part-skim-milk ricotta
    cheese, drained

¼ cup grated orange zest
3 tablespoons granulated sugar
½ teaspoon salt
16 amaretti cookies, crumbled
2 extra-large eggs
½ cup confectioners' sugar

Prepare and stack the crespelle following the instructions for Crespelle with Orange Marmalade Sauce (see Index).

To make the filling, first heat the marsala in a small saucepan. Put the raisins in a small mixing bowl, pour in the marsala, and leave the raisins to soak for about 15 minutes. Drain well.

Preheat the oven to 350°F. With 2 tablespoons of the butter, grease a baking dish measuring 9 by 13 inches.

Put the raisins, ricotta, orange zest, granulated sugar, salt, crumbled amaretti, and eggs in a mixing bowl and stir until combined thoroughly.

One at a time, spread about 3 tablespoons of the filling on half of a crespelle, then fold it over to make a half-moon shape; arrange the filled crespelle slightly overlapping in the buttered baking dish. Melt the remaining butter and drizzle it evenly over the crespelle. Bake them until they are puffed up and bubbling hot, about 15 minutes. Before serving, put the confectioners' sugar in a fine-meshed strainer and tap it over the crespelle to dust them evenly.

Crespelle with Raspberry Jam

This is the way they enjoy crespelle in northeastern Italy. These crespelle make a great simple addition to a breakfast or brunch buffet, accompanied by grilled sausages, griddled ham, or prosciutto. Feel free to substitute whatever type of jam you prefer.

MAKES ABOUT 24 CRESPELLE; 6 TO 8 SERVINGS

Basic Crespelle (see Index)   ½ cup confectioners' sugar
1½ cups raspberry jam

Prepare and stack the crespelle following the instructions for Crespelle with Orange Marmalade Sauce (see Index).

One at a time, spread 1 tablespoon of raspberry jam on each crespelle and then fold the crespelle in half twice to make a wedge shape. As they are filled and folded, arrange the crespelle on a heated serving platter. Put the confectioners' sugar in a fine-meshed strainer and shake it over the crespelle to dust them with the sugar.

Toasted-Hazelnut Waffles with Mascarpone and Nectarines

The rich taste of hazelnuts, which inspires the cooking of Italy's Piedmont region, brings special appeal to these easy waffles. Substitute other juicy fresh fruit such as peaches, plums, or berries as you wish. The actual number of waffles yielded by the recipe will vary with the particular waffle iron you use.

MAKES ABOUT 8 WAFFLES; 4 TO 6 SERVINGS

1 cup whole shelled hazelnuts
1½ cups all-purpose flour
2 tablespoons light brown sugar
1 tablespoon baking powder
½ teaspoon salt
3 extra-large eggs
1½ cups buttermilk

½ cup (¼ pound) unsalted butter, melted
¾ cup mascarpone, at room temperature
3 ripe but firm nectarines, halved, pitted, and thinly sliced
1 cup confectioners' sugar

Preheat the oven to 325°F.

Spread the hazelnuts in a single layer on a baking sheet, put them in the oven, and toast them until light golden, about 10 minutes. Remove the hazelnuts from the oven and reduce the oven temperature to 200°F. While the hazelnuts are still warm, carefully pour them into a folded kitchen towel. Rub the hazelnuts inside the towel to remove their skins.

Preheat a waffle iron following the manufacturer's instructions.

Put the cooled hazelnuts in a food processor fitted with the metal blade. Pulse the machine a few times until the nuts are very coarsely chopped. Transfer half of the nuts to a bowl and set aside.

Process the remaining nuts until they are very finely ground, stopping often to check; do not process so long that they turn to nut butter. Add the flour, brown sugar, baking powder, and salt to the processor and pulse several times, until combined. Add

➤

the eggs, buttermilk, and melted butter and process briefly, just until the batter is blended. Transfer to a bowl and stir in the reserved chopped hazelnuts.

Following the manufacturer's directions, grease the waffle iron's surface with oil or nonstick spray. Add the batter in batches geared to the size of the iron and cook, again following the manufacturer's directions, until the waffles are golden brown. Transfer the waffles to the oven rack to keep warm while cooking the remaining batter.

To serve, arrange the hot waffles on individual serving plates and drizzle or spoon the mascarpone on top. Arrange the nectarine slices on top of the mascarpone. Put the confectioners' sugar in a fine-meshed strainer and tap it over each serving to coat to each guest's taste. Serve immediately.

4

PASTA, RISOTTO, POLENTA, AND SEMOLINA

These grain-based Italian foods—pasta made from the flour of the hard durum wheat known as *semolina*, risotto featuring creamy-textured Arborio or other short-grain rice, and the cornmeal mush known as *polenta*—are normally found on lunch or dinner tables. But each adapts itself effortlessly to morning meals, as the egg-enriched pasta, puddinglike risotto, both sweet and savory simmered and baked polenta, and hearty semolina cereal recipes that follow demonstrate so temptingly.

Spaghetti with Scrambled Eggs,
Slivered Prosciutto, Sun-Dried
Tomatoes, Garlic, and Parmesan

Le Ricette

Spaghetti with Scrambled Eggs, Slivered Prosciutto,
Sun-Dried Tomatoes, Garlic, and Parmesan *84*

Linguine with Smoked Salmon, Scrambled Eggs,
Lemon Zest, and Chives *85*

Farfalle with Crabmeat, Asparagus,
Scrambled Eggs, Garlic, and Herbs *87*

Lasagna with Prosciutto, Ricotta, and
Sautéed Mushrooms *89*

Three-Cheese Lasagna *91*

Risotto Pudding with Mixed Dried Fruit *93*

Cinnamon Risotto with Dried Apples and
Crisp Almonds *95*

Polentina *96*

Maple-Walnut Polenta *97*

Baked Polenta Triangles with Butter and Parmesan *99*

Broiled Parmesan Polenta Fingers with
Tomato Dipping Sauce *100*

Hot Semolina Cereal *101*

Pasta, Risotto, Polenta, and Semolina

PASTA AND EGGS

The classic Italian preparation spaghetti carbonara, with its sauce of egg yolks and bacon, stands as a prime example of how well eggs go with pasta. The following recipes make pasta even more of a morning specialty, increasing the quantity of eggs and adding such embellishments as prosciutto, sun-dried tomatoes, mascarpone, and Parmesan cheese. Feel free to use these recipes as the starting point for your own experiments in breakfast or brunch pasta.

Spaghetti with Scrambled Eggs, Slivered Prosciutto, Sun-Dried Tomatoes, Garlic, and Parmesan

Bold Italian flavors sing out in this simple, quickly prepared mélange.

MAKES 4 TO 6 SERVINGS

1 pound spaghetti or similar pasta
10 extra-large eggs
2 tablespoons milk, half-and-half, or cream
¾ cup freshly grated Parmesan cheese
2 tablespoons unsalted butter
2 tablespoons extra-virgin olive oil

2 garlic cloves, minced
¼ pound very thinly sliced prosciutto, cut crosswise into ¼-inch-wide strips
24 pieces oil-packed sun-dried tomatoes, drained well and cut into ¼-inch-wide strips
¼ cup chopped fresh Italian parsley

Bring a large pot of water to a boil. Add the spaghetti and cook until al dente, following the manufacturer's suggested cooking time.

Meanwhile, in a mixing bowl, beat the eggs and milk together with a fork or whisk until slightly frothy. Beating continuously, sprinkle in the Parmesan cheese. Set aside.

When the pasta is done, drain it and set aside. Immediately heat the butter and olive oil together in a large skillet over medium heat. Add the garlic and sauté until fragrant, about 1 minute. Add the prosciutto and sun-dried tomato slivers, stirring to keep the prosciutto from clumping. Add the pasta and toss briefly to coat. Pour in the egg mixture and stir and toss until the eggs form moist curds that cling to the spaghetti, 3 to 5 minutes more. Serve immediately, garnished with the parsley.

Linguine with Smoked Salmon, Scrambled Eggs, Lemon Zest, and Chives

Smoked salmon and its classic accompaniments find a natural new morning home intertwined with strands of pasta. Relatively little smoked salmon is used here, so seek out the best quality.

MAKES 4 TO 6 SERVINGS

1 pound linguine or other
    pasta strands
10 extra-large eggs
2 tablespoons unsalted butter
2 tablespoons extra-virgin olive oil
2 shallots, minced
¼ cup mascarpone or cream cheese

¼ pound very thinly sliced smoked
    salmon, cut crosswise into
    ¼-inch-wide strips
2 tablespoons grated lemon zest
¼ cup finely chopped fresh chives
Freshly grated Parmesan cheese
Freshly ground black pepper

Bring a large pot of water to a boil. Add the linguine and cook until al dente, following the manufacturer's suggested cooking time.

Meanwhile, in a mixing bowl, beat the eggs with a fork or whisk until slightly frothy. Set aside.

When the pasta is done, drain it and set aside. Immediately heat the butter and olive oil together in a large skillet over medium heat. Add the shallots and sauté until fragrant, about 1 minute. Add the pasta and toss briefly to coat it with the butter-oil mixture. Pour in the eggs, add the mascarpone or cream cheese, and stir and toss the mixture until the cheese has melted and dispersed and the eggs have just begun to form moist curds, about 2 minutes. Add the smoked salmon, lemon zest, and half of the chives and continue cooking and tossing until the eggs have formed more solid curds that cling to the linguine, 1 to 2 minutes more.

Serve immediately, garnished with the remaining chives, and pass freshly grated Parmesan and black pepper for guests to add generously to taste.

Farfalle with Crabmeat, Asparagus, Scrambled Eggs, Garlic, and Herbs

Freshly cooked crabmeat, bought from a good fishmonger or a supermarket with a frequent turnover, will have a sweet, mild flavor that goes beautifully with thinly sliced asparagus and eggs. Farfalle, *the Italian term for bowtie pasta, is a very pretty bite-sized shape that complements the other ingredients, but you may substitute other shapes or strands as you wish.*

Makes 4 to 6 servings

1 pound farfalle
½ pound asparagus, trimmed and
    sliced diagonally ¼ inch thick
10 extra-large eggs
4 tablespoons unsalted butter
1 garlic clove, minced
¼ cup freshly grated Parmesan
    cheese, plus more for serving
2 tablespoons heavy cream

½ pound cooked lump crabmeat,
    picked over to remove any
    bits of shell or cartilage
¼ cup finely chopped fresh chives
2 tablespoons finely chopped fresh
    Italian parsley
Freshly ground black pepper

Bring a large pot of water to a boil. Add the farfalle and cook until al dente, following the manufacturer's suggested cooking time. About 2 minutes before the pasta is done, add the asparagus.

Meanwhile, in a mixing bowl, beat the eggs with a fork or whisk until slightly frothy. Set aside.

When the pasta and asparagus are done, drain and set aside. Immediately melt the butter in a large skillet over medium heat. Add the garlic and sauté until fragrant, about 1 minute. Add the pasta and asparagus and toss briefly to coat them with the butter mixture. Pour in the eggs, add ¼ cup Parmesan and the cream, and stir and toss the mixture until the eggs just have begun to form moist curds, about 2 minutes. Add the crabmeat, chives, and parsley and continue cooking and tossing until the eggs have formed more solid curds that cling to the farfalle, 1 to 2 minutes more.

Serve immediately, passing freshly grated Parmesan and black pepper for guests to add to taste.

BREAKFAST AND BRUNCH LASAGNAS

Lasagna in the morning? That may sound odd. But when you think about some of the classic ingredients of this pasta casserole—mild cheeses such as ricotta, eggs, and wheat (in the form of the broad lasagna noodles)—you come to realize that lasagna may well adapt to the breakfast or brunch table.

That's exactly what I've done with the recipes that follow. These lasagnas include eggs, and I've eliminated some of the heavier ingredients such as beef that you might find in an evening lasagna. Try them as robust brunch courses, and they'll make quite an impression.

I must point out, however, that they do produce a good quantity of lasagna and that portions suited to morning appetites may be somewhat smaller than those served later in the day. With that in mind, you may want to prepare only half the given quantities, using an 8-inch square cake pan. Also note that leftovers store well in the refrigerator or freezer and may be reheated well in a microwave oven. They're even great for lunch or dinner!

Lasagna with Prosciutto, Ricotta, and Sautéed Mushrooms

Light in consistency but flavorful and satisfying, this makes an outstanding brunch dish. The prosciutto is a bit of an extravagance, so make this for a special occasion or substitute less-expensive ham, thinly sliced.

MAKES 12 SERVINGS

2 tablespoons unsalted butter
2 tablespoons olive oil
2 garlic cloves, minced
2 pounds mushrooms, thinly sliced
Salt

¼ cup finely chopped fresh Italian
    parsley
Freshly ground black pepper
1½ pounds part-skim-milk ricotta
    cheese

RISOTTO FOR BREAKFAST AND BRUNCH

The northern Italian specialty known as *risotto* is normally served as a savory starter or side dish for afternoon or evening meals. But the thick, creamy sauce that forms when such short-grained Italian rice varieties as Arborio, Carnaroli, and Vialone Nano give off their surface starch during cooking also makes risotto a natural for the morning, combined with milk, sugar, and other sweet embellishments.

Look for packages of risotto rice in Italian food stores and well-stocked supermarkets. Be sure to use a good, heavy saucepan for cooking the risotto, an essential for holding heat and promoting the slow, even cooking that produces an ideal consistency.

Risotto Pudding with Mixed Dried Fruit

Cooked in milk, sweetened with brown sugar, embellished with mixed dried fruit, spiced with orange zest and a hint of nutmeg, and then chilled in the refrigerator, risotto becomes a seductive pudding that's ideal for a hot-weather breakfast or brunch.

MAKES 6 SERVINGS

1 quart low-fat (1 percent) milk

1 cup water

1 cup short-grained Italian rice (Arborio, Carnaroli, or Vialone Nano)

1 cup chopped mixed dried fruit

½ cup packed dark brown sugar

¼ teaspoon salt

6 tablespoons half-and-half or whole milk

1 tablespoon finely grated orange zest

1 teaspoon pure vanilla extract

¼ teaspoon freshly grated nutmeg

Put the milk in a saucepan over medium heat. As soon as the milk starts to simmer, remove it from the heat and cover.

In another medium-sized, heavy saucepan, bring the water to a boil. Add the rice and, as soon as the water returns to a boil, stir continuously for 2 minutes; the water will become starchy and will quickly be absorbed by the rice. Pour in the hot milk and add the mixed dried fruit, brown sugar, and salt; stir well. Reduce the heat to medium-low and cook, stirring frequently, until the rice is tender but still slightly chewy and the liquid has formed a thick, creamy sauce, about 30 minutes.

When the rice is done, add the half-and-half or whole milk, orange zest, vanilla, and nutmeg. Stir and cook for about 1 minute more. Transfer to a heatproof bowl and let cool, then cover and chill in the refrigerator for 2 to 3 hours before serving.

Cinnamon Risotto with Dried Apples and Crisp Almonds

A classic flavoring combination for oatmeal marries well with risotto in this heartwarming breakfast dish.

MAKES 6 SERVINGS

½ cup slivered almonds
1 quart low-fat (1 percent) milk
3 cinnamon sticks, broken in half
1 cup water
1 cup short-grained Italian rice
    (Arborio, Carnaroli, or
    Vialone Nano)

½ cup packed dark brown sugar
¼ teaspoon salt
1 cup dried apples, coarsely
    chopped
½ cup apple juice
¼ cup half-and-half or whole milk

Preheat the oven to 325°F. Put the almonds in a baking dish and toast in the oven until golden, 5 to 7 minutes.

Put the milk and cinnamon sticks in a saucepan over medium heat. As soon as the milk starts to simmer, remove it from the heat and cover.

In another medium-sized, heavy saucepan, bring the water to a boil. Add the rice and, as soon as the water returns to a boil, stir continuously for 2 minutes; the water will become starchy and will quickly be absorbed by the rice. Pour in the hot milk along with the cinnamon sticks and add the brown sugar and salt; stir well. Reduce the heat to medium-low and cook, stirring frequently, until the rice is tender but still slightly chewy and the liquid has formed a thick, creamy sauce, about 30 minutes.

While the rice is cooking, put the dried apples in a small bowl, pour in the apple juice, and leave to soak.

When the rice is done, drain the apples and add them to the pan along with the half-and-half or whole milk. Stir and cook for 1 to 2 minutes more, until the apple pieces are warmed. Remove and discard the cinnamon sticks and serve hot, ladled into individual serving bowls. Garnish with the toasted almonds.

POLENTA AND SEMOLINA

Start with the Italian ground cornmeal known as *polenta*—the slow-cooking kind, not products labeled "quick-cooking" or "instant"—and you can easily prepare a robust breakfast porridge or baked or broiled polenta shapes that make satisfying accompaniments to egg dishes. If you wish, polenta shapes may also be cut from the vacuum-packed tubes of precooked polenta mush now found in the refrigerated cases or on the shelves of Italian delis and well-stocked markets. And for a change of pace, try hot breakfast porridge made from semolina, the same hard wheat flour Italians traditionally use to make pasta.

Polentina

Although polenta is generally regarded as a savory side dish, in Lombardy they eat the cornmeal porridge for breakfast much as we would eat oatmeal. Although you can buy quick-cooking polenta almost anywhere today, for the most authentic flavor and best consistency look for traditional boxes or packages of slow-cooking polenta in Italian delis and specialty foods stores.

MAKES 6 SERVINGS

2 quarts water
1½ teaspoons salt
2 cups coarsely ground Italian
    polenta
3 tablespoons unsalted butter, cut
    into small cubes

½ cup packed light brown sugar
1 cup whole, low-fat, or nonfat
    milk

In a large, heavy saucepan, bring the water to a boil. Add the salt. Stirring continuously with a sturdy spoon, slowly pour in the polenta.

Reduce the heat to low, cover the pan, and continue cooking, stirring and scraping the bottom frequently, until the polenta is thick and smooth, about 30 minutes.

Spoon the polenta into individual serving bowls. Pass butter, brown sugar, and milk for each person to add to taste.

Maple-Walnut Polenta

Favorite oatmeal additions are also well suited to Italian cornmeal, as this robust morning cereal demonstrates.

MAKES 6 SERVINGS

½ cup coarsely chopped walnut pieces

2 quarts low-fat (1 percent) milk, plus more for serving

½ teaspoon salt

2 cups coarsely ground Italian polenta

½ cup maple syrup, plus more for serving

3 tablespoons unsalted butter, cut into small cubes, plus more for serving

Preheat the oven to 325°F. Put the nuts in a baking dish and toast in the oven until golden, 5 to 7 minutes.

In a large, heavy saucepan over medium heat, bring the milk to a simmer. Add the salt. Stirring continuously with a sturdy spoon, slowly pour in the polenta.

Reduce the heat to low, cover the pan, and continue cooking, stirring and scraping the bottom frequently, until the polenta is thick and smooth, about 30 minutes. Stir in the maple syrup and butter.

Spoon the polenta into individual serving bowls and top with toasted walnuts. Pass more butter, syrup, and milk for guests to add to taste.

Baked Polenta Triangles with Butter and Parmesan

Offer this dish as an accompaniment to robust broiled, sautéed, or baked Italian sausages. To produce a firmer polenta that can be formed into shapes for baking, less water is used than in a standard polenta recipe.

MAKES 4 TO 6 SERVINGS

3 cups water

1 teaspoon salt

1 cup medium-ground polenta

3 tablespoons unsalted
    butter, softened

3 tablespoons freshly grated
    Parmesan cheese

1 tablespoon finely chopped
    fresh chives

In a large, heavy saucepan, bring the water to a boil. Add the salt. Stirring continuously with a sturdy spoon, slowly pour in the polenta.

Reduce the heat to low, cover the pan, and continue cooking, stirring and scraping the bottom frequently, until the polenta is thick, smooth, and relatively stiff, about 10 minutes. Remove the lid and let cool for 5 minutes.

Rinse a large baking sheet with cold water and leave the sheet wet. Spoon the still-warm polenta onto the baking sheet. Rinse a rolling pin with cold water and use it, still wet, to roll out the polenta to an even thickness of about ½ inch. Leave it to cool and solidify completely, about 30 minutes.

Meanwhile, preheat the oven to 375°F. Lightly grease a 12- to 16-inch broilerproof oval baking dish with butter or spray it with nonstick spray.

With a table knife, cut the polenta into triangles about 3 inches per side. Arrange them overlapping slightly in the baking dish. Dot with the softened butter and sprinkle evenly with the Parmesan.

Bake until the polenta is golden brown, about 20 minutes. If the top is not browned to your liking, broil for about 5 minutes. Sprinkle with chives to garnish and serve immediately.

Broiled Parmesan Polenta Fingers with Tomato Dipping Sauce

Serve these as an accompaniment to scrambled or fried eggs or grilled Italian sausages. To produce a firmer polenta that can be formed into shapes for baking, less liquid is used than in a standard polenta recipe.

MAKES 4 TO 6 SERVINGS

1 quart water

1 teaspoon salt

1⅓ cups medium-ground polenta

1 cup freshly grated Parmesan
    cheese

¼ cup extra-virgin olive oil

2 cups Basic Tomato Sauce
    (see Index)

In a large, heavy saucepan, bring the water to a boil. Add the salt. Stirring continuously with a sturdy spoon, slowly pour in the polenta.

Reduce the heat to low, cover the pan, and continue cooking, stirring and scraping the bottom frequently, until the polenta is thick, smooth, and relatively stiff, about 10 minutes. Remove the lid, stir in the Parmesan, and let cool for 5 minutes.

Rinse a large baking sheet with cold water and leave the sheet wet. Spoon the still-warm polenta onto the baking sheet. Rinse a rolling pin with cold water and use it, still wet, to roll out the polenta to an even thickness of about ½ inch. Leave it to cool and solidify completely, about 30 minutes.

Meanwhile, preheat the broiler and brush a large baking sheet with half of the olive oil.

With a table knife, cut the polenta into fingers measuring about 1 by 4 inches. Lift them carefully with a spatula and place them on the oiled baking sheet. Brush their tops with the remaining oil. Broil until their tops are golden brown, 8 to 10 minutes. Flip them gently with a spatula and broil for 8 to 10 minutes more.

Meanwhile, heat the tomato sauce in the microwave or a small saucepan.

Serve the polenta fingers and pass the warm tomato sauce as a dip for eating the fingers by hand or as a sauce to spoon over the fingers.

Hot Semolina Cereal

The hard durum wheat that is ground into the fine flour from which Italians make pasta also becomes a more coarsely ground flour that can be cooked as a robust breakfast cereal. Look for coarse semolina in Italian delis and well-stocked markets. For an even richer flavor, substitute low-fat (1 percent) or skim milk for all or part of the water.

MAKES 6 SERVINGS

9 cups water	6 tablespoons unsalted butter
1 teaspoon salt	Light or dark brown sugar
3 cups coarsely ground semolina	Whole milk or half-and-half

In a large saucepan, bring the water to a boil. Add the salt. Stirring continuously, pour in the semolina. Reduce the heat to low and simmer gently, stirring occasionally, until the cereal is thick, about 25 minutes.

Spoon the semolina into individual heated bowls. Pass butter, brown sugar, and milk or half-and-half for guests to add to taste.

5

BAKED GOODS

The following recipes keep baking simple. Apart from the pizzas, based

on simple yeast-leavened doughs, all of the following baked goods start

with quickly prepared batters, doughs leavened with baking powder,

or store-bought bread. Breads of outstanding quality abound in markets,

delis, and boutique bakeries everywhere today. To serve bread with any Italian-

style breakfast or brunch, I urge you to seek out a good source of rustic, flavorful

Italian-style loaves with dense crumbs and crunchy or chewy crusts, whether

plain or elaborated with such flavorful additions as rosemary, hazelnuts,

or black olives. Look, too, for the yeast-leavened flatbreads

know as *focaccia*, which can be cut into

squares or wedges and eaten

fresh or toasted.

Pizza-Flavored Bruschetta, Bruschetta
with Prosciutto and Melted Fontina, and
Pesto-Asiago Bruschetta

Le Ricette

BAKED GOODS

Bruschettas

These versions of the traditional Italian topped or flavored toasts are ideal to serve with Italian-style egg dishes or morning pastas. For the ideal-sized slices, look for the type of elongated loaf known by the French term *batard*, measuring about 5 inches wide and 3 inches tall, or cut them from a longer but still narrow sourdough or rustic country loaf.

Pizza-Flavored Bruschetta

My son Jake especially loves these toasts, which remind him of one of his favorite foods.

Makes 4 servings

12 slices sourdough or rustic country-style bread, each about ⅓ to ½ inch thick

2 tablespoons olive oil from oil-packed sun-dried tomatoes

1 garlic clove, cut crosswise in half

3 oil-packed sun-dried tomato pieces, drained well and cut into thin slivers

2 tablespoons finely shredded fresh basil leaves

¼ pound mozzarella cheese, shredded (about 1 cup)

Preheat the broiler.

Lightly brush both sides of each bread slice with the olive oil from the sun-dried tomatoes and arrange the slices on a baking sheet. Toast the slices under the broiler until light golden, about 2 minutes per side. Remove the baking sheet from the broiler, leaving the broiler on.

When the bread is cool enough to handle, lightly rub one side of each slice with the cut side of a garlic clove half. Return the slices to the baking sheet garlic-rubbed side up and top them evenly with the sun-dried tomato slivers, shredded basil, and then the shredded mozzarella.

Return the baking sheet to the broiler. Broil just until the cheese has melted and begun to bubble, about 1 minute more. Serve immediately.

Pesto-Asiago Bruschetta

These toasts are especially fragrant and powerfully flavored. Use a little homemade pesto or buy a jar or refrigerated-case container of premade pesto from an Italian deli or well-stocked supermarket.

MAKES 4 SERVINGS

12 slices sourdough or rustic
    country-style bread, each
    about ⅓ to ½ inch thick
2 tablespoons extra-virgin olive oil

2 tablespoons Basic Pesto (see
    Index) or store-bought pesto
3 ounces Asiago cheese, shredded
    (about ¾ cup)

Preheat the broiler.

Lightly brush both sides of each bread slice with the olive oil and arrange the slices on a baking sheet. Toast the slices under the broiler until light golden, about 2 minutes per side. Remove the baking sheet from the broiler, leaving the broiler on.

Spread one side of each bread slice with a little of the pesto, then sprinkle it evenly with the Asiago cheese. Return the baking sheet to the broiler. Broil just until the cheese has melted and begun to bubble, about 1 minute more. Serve immediately.

Bruschetta with Prosciutto and Melted Fontina

The perfect little accompaniment for any kind of egg dish or breakfast pasta, these toasts pack a lot of flavor and texture into every bite. Use less or more garlic as your own tastes and the occasion call for.

MAKES 4 SERVINGS

12 slices sourdough or rustic
   country-style bread, each
   about ⅓ to ½ inch thick
3 tablespoons extra-virgin olive oil
1 garlic clove, cut crosswise in half

6 ounces fontina cheese, shredded
   (about 1½ cups)
12 tissue-thin slices (about
   ¼ pound) prosciutto
Freshly ground black pepper

Preheat the broiler.

Lightly brush both sides of each bread slice with the olive oil and arrange the slices on a baking sheet. Toast the slices under the broiler until light golden, about 2 minutes per side. Remove the baking sheet from the broiler, leaving the broiler on.

When the bread is cool enough to handle, lightly rub both sides of each slice with the cut side of a garlic clove half. Return the slices to the baking sheet and top them evenly with the shredded fontina cheese.

Return the baking sheet to the broiler. Broil just until the cheese has melted and begun to bubble, about 1 minute more.

Remove the baking sheet from the broiler and immediately drape a slice of prosciutto on top of the cheese on each toast. Grind black pepper over the prosciutto and serve immediately.

Parmesan Bruschetta

Perhaps the simplest of morning accompaniments to egg or pasta dishes, these golden toasts impress by delivering the unadulterated taste of good Parmesan cheese. So find a true Parmigiano-Reggiano from Italy and grate it fresh for these toasts. The recipe is very easy to multiply, and you may want to consider making a pile of them—even if you're serving only four people.

MAKES 4 SERVINGS

6 tablespoons unsalted butter, at
room temperature
⅔ cup freshly grated Parmesan
cheese

12 slices sourdough or rustic
country bread, each about
¼ to ⅓ inch thick

Preheat the oven to 375°F.

In a small mixing bowl, use a fork to mash together the butter and Parmesan until blended thoroughly.

Spread the mixture generously on one side of each bread slice, placing them spread side up on a baking sheet. Bake the bread in the oven until crisp and golden brown, about 12 minutes. Transfer to a napkin-lined basket and serve immediately.

BREAKFAST AND BRUNCH PIZZAS

Pause to think a minute, and you'll realize that even a classic pizza is a perfect morning food, providing bread, flavorful tomato sauce, and cheese. Change the toppings a bit to reflect the kinds of foods folks prefer to start the day with, and you'll begin to see how well pizza adapts to breakfast or brunch entertaining.

The glossary of ingredients at the beginning of the book provides basic recipes for both white and whole wheat pizza doughs that you can make easily a day ahead of time and multiply as needed to serve more guests. Here, you'll find five different recipes for suggested topping combinations, each of which provides quantities appropriate for one individually sized pizza or calzone. They are scaled this way not only to make it easier for you to measure out the topping for a single pizza or calzone, but also to reflect the fact that it can be fun to assemble toppings for several different types of pizzas or calzones, letting guests design and bake their own as their personal tastes dictate.

For making pizzas and calzones, it's a good idea to go out and buy a ceramic pizza stone or baker's tiles. Placed on the oven shelf during preheating, they re-create the environment of a baker's oven. When pizza is baked on top of the stone or tiles, the porous ceramic draws moisture from the crust while giving off intense radiant heat, promoting crispness and a well-cooked topping.

Pizza with Smoked Salmon, Mascarpone, Mozzarella, and Eggs

Voluptuous is the word that comes to mind when I think of this pizza, topped with a variation on the classic deli combination of smoked salmon and cream cheese. Buy the best-quality thinly sliced smoked salmon you can find.

MAKES 1 8-INCH PIZZA; 1 SERVING

1 6-ounce ball White or Whole
    Wheat Pizza Dough (see Index)

¼ cup mascarpone, at room
    temperature

1 tablespoon unsalted butter

2 extra-large eggs, lightly beaten

2 ounces mozzarella cheese, shredded
(about ½ cup)

2 ounces thinly sliced smoked salmon

1 teaspoon finely chopped
fresh chives

1 lemon wedge

Freshly ground black pepper

Put a pizza stone, baking tiles, or a baking sheet in the oven and preheat the oven to 500°F.

Sprinkle a work surface with flour. With the heels of your hands, press down on the dough to flatten it, then lift and gently pull it all around to stretch it gradually into a circle 8 to 9 inches in diameter. Use your fingertips to pinch a ½-inch rim around the circle.

If the mascarpone seems too thick to spread, put it in a small glass bowl and microwave briefly. With a spoon, spread the mascarpone evenly within the rim of the pizza dough.

In a small nonstick skillet, melt the butter over low heat. Add the eggs and cook, stirring with a wooden spoon or spatula, only until they form very moist, very soft curds, 1 to 2 minutes. Spread the eggs on top of the pizza and cover them evenly with the shredded mozzarella.

Reduce the oven temperature to 450°F. Slide a wooden pizza paddle, a large spatula, or a rimless baking sheet under the pizza and transfer it to the oven, sliding it onto the preheated stone, tiles, or baking sheet. Bake until the crust is golden brown, 8 to 10 minutes.

Remove the pizza from the oven with the paddle, baking sheet, or spatula. Drape the smoked salmon evenly on top. Use a pizza wheel or a large knife and cut it into four wedges or leave it whole, to be eaten with a knife and fork. Scatter with the chives and serve with a lemon wedge and black pepper to add to taste.

Pizza with Prosciutto, Garlic-Herb Cream Cheese, Jack Cheese, and Eggs

This is a pizza of bold flavors that stand up well to the rich, sweet taste of good-quality prosciutto.

MAKES 1 8-INCH PIZZA; 1 SERVING

1 6-ounce ball White or Whole
    Wheat Pizza Dough
    (see Index)
2 ounces garlic-herb cream cheese
    such as Boursin, at room
    temperature
1 tablespoon unsalted butter

2 extra-large eggs, lightly beaten
2 ounces Monterey Jack cheese,
    shredded (about ½ cup)
2 ounces thinly sliced prosciutto
1 teaspoon finely chopped fresh
    Italian parsley
Freshly ground black pepper

Put a pizza stone, baking tiles, or a baking sheet in the oven and preheat the oven to 500°F.

Sprinkle a work surface with flour. With the heels of your hands, press down on the dough to flatten it, then lift and gently pull it all around to stretch it gradually into a circle 8 to 9 inches in diameter. Use your fingertips to pinch a ½-inch rim around the circle.

With a table knife, spread the garlic-herb cream cheese evenly within the rim of the pizza dough.

In a small nonstick skillet, melt the butter over low heat. Add the eggs and cook, stirring with a wooden spoon or spatula, only until they form very moist, very soft curds, 1 to 2 minutes. Spread the eggs on top of the pizza and cover them evenly with the shredded Monterey Jack cheese.

Reduce the oven temperature to 450°F. Slide a wooden pizza paddle, a large spatula, or a rimless baking sheet under the pizza and transfer it to the oven, sliding it onto the preheated stone, tiles, or baking sheet. Bake until the crust is golden brown, 8 to 10 minutes.

Remove the pizza from the oven with the paddle, baking sheet, or spatula. Drape the prosciutto evenly on top. Use a pizza wheel or a large knife and cut it into four wedges or leave it whole, to be eaten with a knife and fork. Scatter with the parsley and offer a pepper mill for adding black pepper to taste.

Pizza with Pancetta, Eggs, and Provolone

Think of this as a basic Italian-style bacon-and-eggs pizza. If you can't get pancetta, substitute lean thinly sliced bacon.

Makes 1 8-inch pizza; 1 serving

1 6-ounce ball White or Whole Wheat Pizza Dough (see Index)

¼ cup mascarpone, at room temperature

2 tablespoons freshly grated Parmesan cheese

1 ounce thinly sliced pancetta, coarsely chopped

1 tablespoon unsalted butter

2 extra-large eggs, lightly beaten

2 ounces provolone cheese, shredded (about ½ cup)

1 teaspoon finely chopped fresh chives

1 teaspoon finely chopped fresh Italian parsley

Put a pizza stone, baking tiles, or a baking sheet in the oven and preheat the oven to 500°F.

Sprinkle a work surface with flour. With the heels of your hands, press down on the dough to flatten it, then lift and gently pull it all around to stretch it gradually into a circle 8 to 9 inches in diameter. Use your fingertips to pinch a ½-inch rim around the circle.

If the mascarpone seems too thick to spread, put it in a small glass bowl and microwave briefly. Stir in the grated Parmesan. With a spoon, spread the mascarpone-Parmesan mixture evenly within the rim of the pizza dough.

Put the pancetta in a small nonstick skillet over low heat and cook, stirring with a wooden spoon to separate the pieces, until it begins to frizzle, 2 to 3 minutes. Pour off the fat and add the butter. When the butter melts, add the eggs and cook, stirring with a wooden spoon or spatula, only until they form very moist, very soft curds, 1 to 2 minutes. Spread the egg mixture on top of the pizza and cover evenly with the shredded provolone.

Reduce the oven temperature to 450°F. Slide a wooden pizza paddle, a large spatula, or a rimless baking sheet under the pizza and slide it onto the preheated stone, tiles, or baking sheet. Bake until the crust is golden brown, 8 to 10 minutes.

Remove the pizza from the oven with the paddle, baking sheet, or spatula. Use a pizza wheel or a large knife and cut it into four wedges or leave it whole, to be eaten with a knife and fork. Scatter with the chives and parsley and serve.

Vegetarian Breakfast Pizza with Eggs and Sautéed Vegetables

Extra-virgin olive oil and thinly sliced garlic add character to this colorful morning pizza. Feel free to vary the vegetables with whatever is in season.

MAKES 1 8-INCH PIZZA; 1 SERVING

1 6-ounce ball White or Whole Wheat Pizza Dough (see Index)

2 tablespoons extra-virgin olive oil

1 garlic clove, very thinly sliced lengthwise

½ small zucchini, cut into ½-inch-thick slices

½ red bell pepper, stemmed, seeded, and cut into ½-inch squares

¼ small sweet yellow onion, cut into ½-inch dice

2 tablespoons freshly grated Parmesan cheese

1 tablespoon unsalted butter

2 extra-large eggs, lightly beaten

2 ounces mozzarella cheese, shredded (about ½ cup)

1 teaspoon finely shredded fresh basil leaves

1 teaspoon finely chopped fresh chives

1 teaspoon finely chopped fresh Italian parsley

Put a pizza stone, baking tiles, or a baking sheet in the oven and preheat the oven to 500°F.

Sprinkle a work surface with flour. With the heels of your hands, press down on the dough to flatten it, then lift and gently pull it all around to stretch it gradually into a circle 8 to 9 inches in diameter. Use your fingertips to pinch a ½-inch rim around the circle.

Heat the olive oil in a nonstick skillet over medium-high heat. Add the garlic, zucchini, bell pepper, and onion and sauté until the vegetables just begin to turn golden,

4 to 5 minutes. Distribute the vegetables and their oil evenly over the pizza dough and sprinkle evenly with the Parmesan.

Reduce the heat to low and add the butter to the skillet. When it melts, add the eggs and cook, stirring with a wooden spoon or spatula, only until they form very moist, very soft curds, 1 to 2 minutes. Spread the eggs on top of the vegetables and cover them evenly with the shredded mozzarella.

Reduce the oven temperature to 450°F. Slide a wooden pizza paddle, a large spatula, or a rimless baking sheet under the pizza and transfer it to the oven, sliding it onto the preheated stone, tiles, or baking sheet. Bake until the crust is golden brown, 8 to 10 minutes.

Remove the pizza from the oven with the paddle, baking sheet, or spatula. Use a pizza wheel or a large knife and cut it into four wedges or leave it whole, to be eaten with a knife and fork. Scatter with the basil, chives, and parsley and serve.

Morning Calzone Stuffed with Sausage, Eggs, and Sun-Dried Tomatoes

Any of the preceding morning pizzas can be transformed into a calzone, the traditional Italian-style savory turnover, simply by following the filling and shaping instructions in this recipe. However, calzones work best when they hold chunkier fillings that might tumble off a slice of pizza, such as the combination given here.

MAKES 1 8-INCH CALZONE; 1 SERVING

1 6-ounce ball White or Whole Wheat Pizza Dough (see Index)

¼ cup mascarpone, at room temperature

2 tablespoons freshly grated Parmesan cheese

3 ounces mozzarella cheese, shredded (about ¾ cup)

1 spicy or sweet fresh Italian sausage, about ¼ pound

1 tablespoon unsalted butter

2 extra-large eggs, lightly beaten

4 oil-packed sun-dried tomato pieces, drained well and cut into ¼-inch-wide slivers

1 teaspoon finely shredded fresh basil leaves

1 teaspoon finely chopped fresh chives

1 teaspoon finely chopped fresh Italian parsley

Put a pizza stone, baking tiles, or a baking sheet in the oven and preheat the oven to 500°F.

Sprinkle a work surface with flour. With the heels of your hands, press down on the dough to flatten it, then lift and gently pull it all around to stretch it gradually into a circle 8 to 9 inches in diameter.

If the mascarpone seems too thick to spread, put it in a small glass bowl and microwave briefly. Stir in the grated Parmesan. With a spoon, spread the mascarpone-Parmesan mixture evenly over the pizza dough, leaving a border about ½ inch wide. Sprinkle half of the shredded mozzarella evenly over half of the mascarpone-Parmesan mixture.

With the tip of a small sharp knife, slit the casing and remove it from the sausage. Pinch off ½-inch chunks of sausage and drop them into a small nonstick skillet over low heat. Cook, stirring occasionally, until the sausage loses its pink color and begins to brown, about 5 minutes.

Pour off the fat and add the butter. When the butter melts, add the eggs and cook, stirring with a wooden spoon or spatula, only until they form very moist, very soft curds, 1 to 2 minutes. Spread the eggs and sausage on top of the mozzarella. Sprinkle with the sun-dried tomatoes, basil, chives, and parsley and top with the remaining mozzarella.

Carefully fold the other half of the dough over the topped side to enclose the filling. With your fingertips, carefully pinch the edges of dough securely together all along the rim to seal in the filling. With the tip of a sharp knife, slit a small air vent in the top of the calzone.

Reduce the oven temperature to 450°F. Slide a wooden pizza paddle, a large spatula, or a rimless baking sheet under the calzone and transfer it to the oven, sliding it onto the preheated stone, tiles, or baking sheet. Bake until the crust is golden brown, 8 to 10 minutes.

Remove the calzone from the oven with the paddle, baking sheet, or spatula. Serve it whole, to be eaten with a knife and fork, or use a large, sharp knife to cut it crosswise in half, taking care to avoid the steam when you cut it open.

BISCOTTI

Their name literally meaning "twice cooked," classic Italian biscotti are cookies that are baked once as a large loaf and then again as slices to give them their signature crisp, crunchy texture. Many cafés today offer excellent commercially made biscotti, of which those studded with almonds or hazelnuts are most common.

The two recipes that follow offer unique twists on the biscotti concept, one sweet, one savory. Both are sized a bit larger than those with which you might be familiar, providing a more substantial portion for a morning meal.

Chocolate, Orange, and Honey Biscotti

These offer a grown-up, sweet taste that even kids at the brunch table will enjoy. The orange and honey give the biscotti a striking golden color. Serve them with Caffe Latte or Cappuccino (see Index) at the end of a breakfast or brunch or as a midmorning treat.

MAKES ABOUT 3 DOZEN

2 cups all-purpose flour
1 teaspoon baking powder
½ teaspoon baking soda
½ teaspoon salt
½ cup unsalted butter, at room temperature

½ cup orange-blossom honey
2 extra-large eggs
3 tablespoons grated orange zest
1 tablespoon fresh orange juice
1½ cups semisweet chocolate chips

Preheat the oven to 350°F. Spray two baking sheets with nonstick spray.

In a bowl, stir together the flour, baking powder, baking soda, and salt. Set aside.

Put the butter, honey, eggs, orange zest, and orange juice in a large mixing bowl. Beat with an electric mixer set on high speed until smooth, about 30 seconds. Add the flour mixture, reduce the speed to low, and beat just until combined. Stir in the chocolate chips. Cover and refrigerate until well chilled, about 3 hours.

➤

Divide the dough in half and transfer each half to one of the prepared baking sheets, firmly patting and shaping it into a log about 2 inches wide and 1 inch high.

Bake the logs until firm, about 30 minutes; they will spread a little as they bake. Remove from the oven and let cool for about 10 minutes; reduce the oven temperature to 300°F.

With a wide spatula, carefully transfer the logs to a cutting board. With a serrated bread knife, cut the logs diagonally into ½-inch-thick slices. As you cut them, arrange the slices cut sides down on the baking sheets.

Return the slices to the oven and bake them until their undersides are golden brown, about 7 minutes more. Remove them from the oven, turn them over with the spatula, and bake until the other sides are brown, another 7 minutes or so.

With the spatula, transfer the biscotti to wire racks to cool completely. Store in an airtight container at room temperature for up to 2 weeks.

Pizza Biscotti

In developing this recipe, I aimed to capture in crisp biscotti the flavor combination of a cheese-and-tomato pizza. The savory, fragrant biscotti that resulted make an outstanding accompaniment to egg dishes or pastas at breakfast or brunch. They gain a beautiful, rosy color from the tomato paste.

MAKES ABOUT 3 DOZEN

2 cups all-purpose flour
1 cup freshly grated Parmesan
    cheese
1 tablespoon sugar
2 teaspoons dried oregano,
    crumbled
1½ teaspoons baking powder
½ teaspoon baking soda
1 teaspoon salt

6 tablespoons unsalted butter, at
    room temperature
2½ tablespoons extra-virgin
    olive oil
2 tablespoons double-concentrate
    tomato paste
2 extra-large eggs
2 garlic cloves, pressed through a
    garlic press

Preheat the oven to 350°F. Spray two baking sheets with nonstick spray.

In a bowl, stir together the flour, Parmesan, sugar, oregano, baking powder, baking soda, and salt. Set aside.

Put the butter, olive oil, and tomato paste in a large mixing bowl. Beat with an electric mixer set on high speed until light and fluffy, about 1 minute. One at a time, add the eggs, beating after each addition until light and fluffy, about 2 minutes total. Reduce the speed to low and briefly beat in the garlic until incorporated. Add the flour mixture, keep the speed on low, and beat just until combined and a crumbly dough begins to form.

With your hands, gather up the dough, pressing it together to form a solid ball. Divide it in half and transfer each half to one of the prepared baking sheets, firmly patting and shaping it into a log about 3 inches wide and ¾ inch high.

➤

Bake the logs until firm, about 30 minutes, switching the position of the baking sheets halfway through baking; the logs will spread a little as they bake. Remove from the oven and let cool for about 5 minutes; reduce the oven temperature to 300°F.

With a wide spatula, carefully transfer the logs to a cutting board. With a serrated bread knife, cut the logs diagonally into ½-inch-thick slices. As you cut them, arrange the slices cut sides down on the baking sheets.

Return the slices to the oven and bake them until their undersides are golden brown, about 15 minutes more. Remove them from the oven, turn them over with the spatula, and bake until the other sides are brown, another 15 minutes or so.

With the spatula, transfer the biscotti to wire racks to cool completely. Store in an airtight container at room temperature for up to 2 weeks.

QUICK BREADS

Muffins, pound cake, scones, and biscuits—all favorite morning breads—adapt well to Italian-style embellishments such as polenta, espresso, mascarpone, sun-dried tomatoes, or pine nuts. Leavening with baking powder helps them come together quickly, leaving you more time to enjoy the pleasures of the meal. For the best results, don't use baking powder that has been open for more than 3 to 4 months; it will lose its strength and should be replaced with a fresh container.

Lemon Polenta Muffins

Sweet with the flavor of Italian cornmeal and lemon, these muffins turn out a sunshine golden color, perfect for the morning table. Using instant polenta helps ensure that they have a more tender texture; coarse-grained, slow-cooking polenta will give them a rather crunchy crumb.

MAKES ABOUT 16 MUFFINS

2 cups packed light brown sugar
6 tablespoons unsalted butter, at
    room temperature
¼ cup grated lemon zest
    (about 4 lemons)
6 extra-large eggs

2 cups all-purpose flour
1 cup instant polenta
3 tablespoons baking powder
1 teaspoon baking soda
½ teaspoon salt
½ cup milk

Preheat the oven to 350°F. Grease 16 muffin cups using nonstick spray.

In a mixing bowl, use a handheld electric mixer on low speed to combine the brown sugar, butter, and lemon zest, about 1 minute. One at a time, beat in the eggs.

In a separate bowl, stir together the flour, polenta, baking powder, baking soda, and salt. Stir about one-fourth of the flour mixture into the creamed ingredients, then stir in about one-fourth of the milk; repeat until all the ingredients are just combined.

Distribute the mixture evenly among the greased muffin cups. Bake until well risen and golden and a wooden toothpick inserted into the center of one comes out clean, about 25 minutes. Leave them in the tin for 2 to 3 minutes to cool before removing and serving. Freeze any leftover muffins in airtight bags for up to 2 months and reheat gently in the oven or microwave.

Mocha Chip Muffins

The flavors of espresso coffee and chocolate blend seductively in these intense muffins. You'll find jars of instant espresso powder in well-stocked food stores and Italian delis.

MAKES 12 MUFFINS

1½ cups all-purpose flour

1 cup sugar

½ cup unsweetened cocoa powder

2 teaspoons instant espresso powder

2 teaspoons baking powder

½ teaspoon salt

1 cup evaporated milk

1 extra-large egg, lightly beaten

¼ cup vegetable oil

1 teaspoon pure vanilla extract

½ cup semisweet chocolate chips

Preheat the oven to 350°F. Spray 12 muffin cups with nonstick spray.

In a mixing bowl, stir together the flour, sugar, cocoa powder, espresso powder, baking powder, and salt. In another bowl, stir together the evaporated milk, egg, vegetable oil, and vanilla until well blended. Add the dry ingredients and stir just until evenly blended. Stir in the chocolate chips.

Spoon the batter evenly into the prepared muffin cups. Bake until a toothpick inserted into the center of a muffin comes out without batter clinging to it (although a little melted chocolate might cling), about 20 minutes.

Remove the muffin tin from the oven and place it on a wire rack to cool for about 5 minutes. Invert the tin to remove the muffins. Serve them in a napkin-lined bowl or basket. Freeze any leftover muffins in airtight bags for up to 2 months and reheat gently in the oven or microwave.

Polenta Mascarpone Pound Cake

Rich and buttery, this classic cake gains Italian inspiration from the inclusion of quick-cooking polenta, mascarpone, and a hint of almond. Serve it sliced with coffee. You can also lightly toast the slices under the broiler and use them as a base for lightly sweetened fresh fruit.

MAKES 1 9-BY-5-INCH LOAF; 8 TO 12 SERVINGS

½ cup (¼ pound) unsalted butter, plus 1 tablespoon for greasing, at room temperature

1½ cups sifted cake flour, plus 1 tablespoon for flouring

½ cup quick-cooking polenta

½ teaspoon baking powder

½ cup mascarpone, at room temperature

1⅓ cups sugar

1 teaspoon almond extract

½ teaspoon pure vanilla extract

4 extra-large eggs, at room temperature

Preheat the oven to 325°F. Grease a 9-by-5-inch loaf pan with 1 tablespoon of the butter. Add 1 tablespoon of the flour to the pan and tilt and tap the pan to coat its greased bottom and sides with the flour; tap out any excess into the sink.

In a mixing bowl, stir together the 1½ cups cake flour, the polenta, and the baking powder. Put the ½ cup butter and the mascarpone in another mixing bowl and, using an electric mixer on medium speed, beat for about 30 seconds. Beating continuously, add the sugar a little at a time and then continue beating until the mixture is light and fluffy, 5 to 7 minutes more. Still beating, add the almond and vanilla extracts. Then, one at a time, add the eggs, beating for about 1 minute after each addition.

A third at a time, add the dry ingredients, beating in each addition at low speed until smoothly blended. Use a rubber spatula to scrape down the sides of the bowl during beating. With the help of the spatula, transfer the batter to the loaf pan.

Bake the cake until it is golden brown and a wooden toothpick inserted into its center comes out clean, 60 to 70 minutes. Move the pan to a wire rack to cool for about 10 minutes. Carefully run a table knife around the sides of the cake to loosen it from the pan. Place the wire rack on top of the pan and, using pot holders or oven mitts, invert pan and rack together to unmold the cake. Turn the unmolded cake over again so its curved side is on top and let cool completely before slicing crosswise and serving. Store in an airtight container at cool room temperature for up to 2 days.

Panettone-Style Scones and Buttermilk, Sun-Dried Tomato, Pine Nut , and Rosemary Scones

Panettone-Style Scones

The mixed candied fruit and hint of amaretto give these easy-to-make morning breads the look and taste of a classic packaged or bakery-bought Italian panettone.

MAKES ABOUT 8 SCONES

½ cup chopped mixed candied fruit

2 tablespoons amaretto liqueur

2 cups all-purpose flour

¼ cup sugar

1 tablespoon baking powder

¼ teaspoon salt

1 cup plus 2 tablespoons heavy cream

Put the candied fruit in a small bowl, breaking up the pieces with your fingers. Sprinkle the amaretto over the fruit and stir briefly. Leave the fruit to soak up the liqueur for 15 minutes.

Meanwhile, preheat the oven to 425°F. Lightly spray a baking sheet with nonstick spray.

In a mixing bowl, stir together the flour, sugar, baking powder, and salt. Add the heavy cream and the candied fruit–amaretto mixture to the bowl and stir with a fork just until the dry ingredients are moistened uniformly. Knead the dough briefly in the bowl, gently squeezing it with both hands just until it feels fairly smooth and holds together.

Transfer the dough to a lightly floured work surface and roll it out to a thickness of about ¾ inch. Use a floured 3-inch round cutter to cut out the scones, transferring them to the baking sheet about 2 inches apart. Bake until the scones are golden, 12 to 15 minutes. Check carefully toward the end of the baking time to make sure their bottoms aren't burning; if they look like they're getting too dark, flip them over with a spatula before continuing baking. Serve hot from the oven or lukewarm, in a napkin-lined and -covered bowl or basket to keep them warm.

Buttermilk, Sun-Dried Tomato, Pine Nut, and Rosemary Scones

This unusual, fragrant, savory bread is baked in the traditional wedge-shaped style favored in Scotland, birthplace of the scone. But the presence of sun-dried tomatoes, pine nuts, and a hint of rosemary gives it true Italian style. Serve these scones with eggs, sausages, or prosciutto.

MAKES 8 SCONES

2½ cups all-purpose flour

3 tablespoons sugar

4 teaspoons baking powder

1 teaspoon dried rosemary, finely crumbled

½ teaspoon salt

1 cup buttermilk

¼ cup pine nuts

¼ cup oil-packed sun-dried tomato pieces, drained well, patted dry with paper towels, and cut into ¼-inch slices

3 tablespoons extra-virgin olive oil

1 extra-large egg, lightly beaten

Preheat the oven to 425°F. Lightly spray a baking sheet with nonstick spray.

In a mixing bowl, stir together the flour, sugar, baking powder, rosemary, and salt. Add the buttermilk, pine nuts, sun-dried tomatoes, olive oil, and egg; stir with a fork just until the dry ingredients are moistened uniformly. Knead the dough briefly in the bowl, gently squeezing it with both hands just until it feels fairly smooth and holds together.

Transfer the dough to the prepared baking sheet and pat it into a uniform, smooth round about ¾ inch thick. With a table knife, press down through the dough to mark it into eight equal wedges, but do not separate them. Bake for 10 to 12 minutes, until the dough is golden on its underside (check by using a spatula to lift an edge). Remove the baking sheet from the oven, leaving the oven on.

Wait a few minutes, then use a table knife to carefully cut the wedges apart. With a spatula, separate the wedges and gently flip them over. Return to the oven and bake until the wedges are completely cooked through and the scones are golden brown, 3 to 5 minutes more.

Scones with Candied Chestnuts

Come the holiday season, some Italian bakers like to include candied chestnuts in baked goods such as panettone. Look in a specialty foods store for jars of crystallized or candied chestnuts.

MAKES ABOUT 8 SCONES

½ cup candied chestnuts cut into
    ¼-inch dice

2 tablespoons brandy or cognac

2 tablespoons finely grated orange zest

2 cups all-purpose flour

⅓ cup sugar

1 tablespoon baking powder

¼ teaspoon salt

1 cup plus 2 tablespoons heavy cream

Put the chestnuts in a small bowl, breaking up the pieces with your fingers. Sprinkle the brandy or cognac and the orange zest over the chestnuts and stir briefly. Leave the chestnuts to soak for 15 minutes.

Meanwhile, preheat the oven to 425°F. Lightly spray a baking sheet with nonstick spray.

In a mixing bowl, stir together the flour, sugar, baking powder, and salt. Add the heavy cream and the chestnut-brandy mixture to the bowl and stir with a fork just until the dry ingredients are moistened uniformly. Knead the dough briefly in the bowl, gently squeezing it with both hands just until it feels fairly smooth and holds together.

Transfer the dough to a lightly floured work surface and roll it out to a thickness of about ¾ inch. Use a floured 3-inch round cutter to cut out the scones, transferring them to the baking sheet about 2 inches apart. Bake until the scones are golden, 12 to 15 minutes. Check carefully toward the end of the baking time to make sure their bottoms aren't burning; if they look like they're getting too dark, flip them over with a spatula before continuing baking. Serve hot from the oven or lukewarm, in a napkin-lined and -covered bowl or basket to keep them warm.

Toasted Pine Nut-Honey Butter, Fresh Basil-
Lemon Butter, Toasted Hazelnut-Orange Butter,
and Parmesan-Pepper Butter

Parmesan-Pepper Butter

This is an elegant and easy little spread to accompany warm biscuits or toast served with egg dishes.

MAKES 8 TO 12 SERVINGS

½ cup (¼ pound) unsalted butter, at room temperature

¼ cup freshly grated Parmesan cheese

1 teaspoon freshly ground black pepper

Put the butter, Parmesan, and pepper in a mixing bowl and mash them together with a fork until thoroughly blended.

With a rubber spatula, scrape the mixture from the bowl and pack into individual little butter dishes. Cover them with plastic wrap and refrigerate. Alternatively, mold the butter into a cylinder about 1 inch in diameter, roll it up in wax paper or plastic wrap, and refrigerate.

Half an hour before serving, remove the butter from the refrigerator. If using the cylinder of butter, cut it while still cold into individual portions or pats, arranging them decoratively on a serving dish or on individual bread plates. Let the butter come to room temperature before serving with toast.

6

MEATS

At other times of day, meat is usually the

star of a meal. Breakfast meats, however, serve

more as an accompaniment to eggs or pasta or, in the

European style, as an embellishment for good-quality bread enjoyed

with a cup of coffee. As the recipes that follow show, however, meats can

sometimes regain their leading role on the morning table when they're dressed in Italian-

style trappings. But you don't necessarily even need a recipe to add meats to

an Italian-style breakfast or brunch menu. Scan the Italian cold cuts in

a deli case and consider expanding your breakfast or brunch

offerings with a platter of thinly sliced cured

sausages such as garlicky salami, smooth

and rich mortadella, smoke-dried

soppressata, or spicy

pepperoni.

Pan-Roasted Italian Sausages
with Red and Green Grapes

LE RICETTE

Pan-Roasted Italian Sausages with Red and Green Grapes

Even though these are easy to prepare, they make an especially festive presentation. Look in a well-stocked butcher shop or Italian deli for good-quality fresh Italian sausages made from the traditional pork or from turkey or even chicken. The recipe works well with either chile-laced spicy sausages or the sweeter kind that are usually seasoned with whole fennel seeds. Taste a grape of each type before you buy them to make sure they're good and sweet.

MAKES 6 TO 8 SERVINGS

2 pounds fresh Italian sausages, about ¼ pound each

1 to 1½ cups dry to medium-dry white wine such as Chardonnay or Pinot Grigio

1 cup stemmed seedless sweet red grapes

1 cup stemmed seedless sweet green grapes

1 tablespoon finely chopped fresh Italian parsley

1 tablespoon finely chopped fresh chives

Preheat the oven to 425°F.

With a fork, puncture each sausage in two or three places. Arrange the sausages in a baking dish large enough to hold them in a single layer without touching. Pour 1 cup of the wine into the baking dish. Put the dish in the oven and bake the sausages for about 25 minutes, turning them once about halfway through, until most of the wine has evaporated and the sausages have begun to brown. If the wine disappears too quickly, add a little more to keep the bottom of the baking dish slightly moist.

While the sausages are cooking, carefully use the tip of a small sharp knife to puncture the skin of each grape.

Scatter the grapes all around the sausages and continue baking until the sausages are well browned and the grapes are heated through, about 10 minutes more. Garnish with the parsley and chives. Serve the sausages and grapes straight from the baking dish if you like, using a fork to transfer the sausages to serving plates and a large spoon to scoop up the grapes.

Italian Sausage Patties Pizzaiola

This delicious, unconventional way of preparing Italian sausage makes an especially attractive presentation and is a very nice companion to simple scrambled eggs. The recipe works well using either sweet or spicy fresh Italian sausages, made from pork, turkey, or chicken. In place of each basil leaf, try a dab of pesto bought in the market or prepared yourself using the recipe in this book (see Index).

MAKES 6 TO 12 SERVINGS

2¼ pounds fresh Italian sausage, in links or bulk

¾ cup Basic Tomato Sauce (see Index)

12 whole fresh basil leaves

½ pound mozzarella cheese, shredded (about 2 cups)

Preheat the oven to 400°F. Place one or more wire racks in a shallow baking pan.

If using sausage links, slit, peel off, and discard their casings. Form the sausage meat into 12 equal patties of about 3 ounces each, patting them firmly to an even ½-inch thickness and placing them on the wire rack.

Bake the sausage patties in the oven for about 15 minutes, turning them once, until their juices run clear. Turn off the oven and turn on the broiler. Remove the pan from the oven and spread 1 tablespoon of the tomato sauce on top of each patty. Place a basil leaf on top of the sauce and cover the leaf and sauce with shredded mozzarella. Return the patties to the broiler and broil just until the cheese melts, 2 to 3 minutes.

Pancetta Pinwheels

Utterly simple though these spirals of Italian bacon are, they make quite an impression at a special breakfast or brunch, especially when served alongside or leaning against scrambled or fried eggs. The key to preparing them is just a bit of care. An unsmoked form of bacon, pancetta is made by seasoning a flat piece of pork belly with black pepper and sometimes garlic and other spices, then rolling it up tightly and curing it with salt. Most Italian delis or well-stocked supermarkets that carry it will cut it up in its still-rolled-up form, yielding spiral-shaped slices. Ask whoever slices it for you to take care to keep the spirals intact and layer them with wax paper or plastic wrap. Then, at home, handle them carefully to maintain their striking shape during cooking. Using a nonstick skillet and adding a little olive oil for insurance helps keep the sometimes delicate slices from sticking.

MAKES 4 TO 6 SERVINGS

1 to 2 tablespoons extra-virgin olive oil

12 thin slices pancetta

1 tablespoon finely chopped fresh Italian parsley (optional)

Put the oil in one or two nonstick skillets large enough to hold the pancetta slices easily in a single layer without touching. Very carefully arrange the spiral-shaped slices on the bottom of the skillet or skillets.

Cook over medium-low heat until the pancetta spirals are crisp but not overly browned, 8 to 10 minutes, using a spatula or kitchen tongs to turn them every 2 to 3 minutes after they start sizzling. If the pancetta seems to be browning too quickly, reduce the heat to low. Drain on paper towels and serve while still hot, garnished with a little parsley if you like.

Griddled Prosciutto

Normally, prosciutto, the fabled cured raw ham of Parma and other northern Italian regions, is enjoyed uncooked in tissue-thin slices that highlight its sweet-salty flavor and velvety texture. But very quick searing on a hot griddle or in a hot skillet subtly enhances the ham's sweetness and gives it a meatier texture often appreciated alongside eggs on the breakfast plate. The cooking process is so quick and simple that it can be managed with ease just before serving a breakfast or brunch main course.

Makes 4 to 6 servings

1 tablespoon unsalted butter
1 tablespoon extra-virgin olive oil
12 thin slices prosciutto

1 tablespoon finely chopped fresh
   Italian parsley

Preheat a griddle or large skillet over medium–high heat. Add the butter and oil, using a spoon or fork to swirl the butter around as it melts, coating the surface. As soon as the butter has melted, add the prosciutto slices in a single layer, in batches if necessary. Sear them for no more than 20 to 30 seconds per side, just until they frizzle a bit and begin to change in color. Remove the slices to a heated platter, garnish with parsley, and serve immediately.

7

FRUITS AND VEGETABLES

Side dishes though they usually are at breakfast or brunch, fruit and vegetable dishes have the power to make a big impact on the success of a meal. Consider the accompaniments that follow. Some, such as simple presentations of blood oranges, berries, melons, or figs, provide ideal starters for more elaborate brunches. Fruit dishes can also make spectacular brunch desserts, as evidenced by the peach-topped pound cake, creamy panna cotta, and two fruit tarts included in this chapter. Others, most notably the recipes for potatoes, mushrooms, and tomatoes, elevate even the simplest of egg preparations with which they are served.

Honeyed Figs with Prosciutto

LE RICETTE

Honeyed Figs with Prosciutto

Honey-sweet and lusciously juicy, figs partner perfectly with the velvety texture and sublime flavor of Italy's renowned cured raw ham in this knife-and-fork brunch dish, a fine starter before eggs or a pasta. To help you handle the prosciutto more easily, ask for it to be sliced very thinly, with each slice on a separate sheet of wax paper or plastic wrap. A light drizzle of honey and a spritz of lime or lemon magically marries their flavors.

MAKES 4 TO 6 SERVINGS

12 plump ripe fresh figs

12 tissue-thin slices prosciutto

¼ cup honey

1 lime or lemon, cut into wedges

Fresh mint sprigs for garnish

Cut each fig lengthwise into quarters. Carefully drape the prosciutto slices on individual chilled serving plates. Arrange the figs, cut sides up, on top and drizzle them lightly with the honey, about 1 teaspoon for four fig pieces.

Place a lime or lemon wedge on each plate for each guest to squeeze over the figs to taste. Garnish with mint sprigs and serve.

Fresh Pears with Gorgonzola

With their musky aroma and hints of honey, pears have a natural affinity for Italy's pungent blue cheese, Gorgonzola. This morning side dish combines the two with the utmost of simplicity.

MAKES 4 TO 8 SERVINGS

4 firm but ripe sweet eating pears such as Bartlett, Bosc, Comice, or Winter Nelis

2 tablespoons fresh lemon juice

6 ounces Gorgonzola cheese (or other good-quality blue-veined variety)

Fresh mint sprigs for garnish

Quarter the pears, cut out their cores and stems, and cut each quarter lengthwise into three or four thin wedges. Immediately put the wedges into a mixing bowl with the lemon juice and toss very gently to coat them and keep them from oxidizing.

Arrange the pear slices in attractive fan patterns on individual chilled serving plates. Crumble the Gorgonzola cheese evenly over the slices. Garnish with mint and serve.

Blood Oranges with Honey

My wife and I enjoyed just such a simple, beautiful breakfast dish one morning while honey-mooning in northern Italy on the shore of Lago Maggiore. I've added the hint of cinnamon, which seems to complement the robust tang of blood oranges. The presentation would work just as nicely with regular oranges, but the visual impact won't be as stunning as that delivered by the orange-red fruit.

MAKES 4 SERVINGS

6 blood oranges (1¾ to 2 pounds total)

4 teaspoons honey
Ground cinnamon

To prepare the oranges, first cut a slice off the top and bottom of each fruit just thick enough to expose the pulp beneath its membrane. Then, steadying each fruit on a cutting board on one of its cut ends, carefully slice off the peel in thick strips, following the fruit's contour. Cut each orange crosswise into ¼-inch-thick slices. Alternatively, holding the fruit over a bowl, carefully use a small, sharp knife to cut down along the membrane on either side of each segment, freeing the segment and letting it drop into the bowl.

Arrange the slices or segments on individual small dessert or fruit plates. Drizzle with the honey and dust very lightly with a tiny pinch of cinnamon per serving.

Citrus Salad with Vin Santo and Mint

Just a tiny bit of extra effort turns popular morning fruit into an elegant dish to serve at breakfast or brunch. Vin Santo, the famed dessert wine of central Italy, adds a hint of nutty flavor along with extra sweetness.

MAKES 4 TO 6 SERVINGS

¼ cup fresh mint leaves

½ cup Vin Santo

4 sweet seedless oranges

1 ruby, pink, or white grapefruit

Fresh mint sprigs for garnish

With your hands, firmly crush the mint leaves. Put them in a small nonreactive bowl or a large glass and pour the Vin Santo over them. Leave to soak for at least 30 minutes.

With a citrus zester, remove the zest from one of the oranges in thin strips or remove the zest using a swivel-bladed vegetable peeler, taking care to avoid any of the bitter white pith, and then use a small, sharp knife to cut the zest crosswise into thin strips. Reserve the zest.

To segment the oranges and grapefruit, first cut a slice off the top and bottom of each fruit just thick enough to expose the pulp beneath its membrane. Then, steadying a fruit on a cutting board on one of its cut ends, carefully slice off the peel in strips just thick enough to remove the outer membrane from each segment, following the fruit's contour. Holding the fruit over a mixing bowl, carefully use a small, sharp knife to cut down along the membrane on either side of each segment, freeing the segment and letting it drop into the bowl.

Hold a strainer over the bowl and pour the Vin Santo through it to remove the crushed mint leaves; discard the leaves. Add the reserved orange zest and stir gently to mix. Cover with plastic wrap and refrigerate until chilled, at least 1 hour. Garnish the salad with mint sprigs before serving.

Balsamic Strawberries

Wait to make this simple recipe in early summer when strawberries are at their juiciest, sweetest peak. Serve them on their own to start a brunch or as an accompaniment to breakfast breads. Or, if you want to be especially decadent, offer them at the end of a brunch over scoops of good-quality vanilla ice cream or frozen yogurt.

MAKES 4 TO 6 SERVINGS

½ cup good-quality balsamic
vinegar

½ cup sugar

2 pints ripe strawberries

¼ cup mascarpone, at room
temperature

2 teaspoons finely chopped fresh
mint leaves

Put the vinegar and sugar in a small nonreactive saucepan and stir over low heat just until the sugar dissolves. Transfer to a nonreactive bowl, cover, and refrigerate until cool, at least 30 minutes.

About 30 minutes before serving, rinse and hull the strawberries. Cut small ones lengthwise into halves, larger ones lengthwise into quarters. In a nonreactive mixing bowl, toss the berries together with the sweetened balsamic vinegar. Let them sit at room temperature for at least 15 minutes before spooning them into individual serving bowls, topped with dollops of mascarpone and garnished with mint.

Mixed Melon Salad with Marsala

The celebrated dessert wine of Sicily is a classic companion for ripe, sweet melon. For an attractive and easy presentation, I scoop the melon into bite-sized balls that are tossed together and marinated briefly with the marsala.

MAKES 8 TO 12 SERVINGS

1 large ripe cantaloupe
1 large ripe honeydew melon
6 tablespoons marsala
1 tablespoon sugar (optional)

2 tablespoons finely shredded
lemon zest
Fresh mint leaves

Halve the melons and scoop out their seeds. With a melon baller, scoop out the flesh, transferring the melon balls to a mixing bowl. Sprinkle in the marsala, toss gently with a spoon, and taste. If it seems that the melons could taste a little sweeter, sprinkle in some of the sugar. Add the lemon zest and toss gently again. Cover the bowl with plastic wrap and refrigerate for 1 to 2 hours.

To serve, spoon the melon balls and the juices that have accumulated into individual chilled serving bowls. Garnish with mint leaves.

Peaches in Red Wine

Simple, elegant, and as striking in its vivid colors as it is in its flavors, this wonderful fruit dish begs for the ripest of fresh summer peaches. You can also make it with nectarines. Serve to end a brunch or as an offering on a buffet.

MAKES 6 TO 8 SERVINGS

8 large ripe but firm sweet freestone peaches

6 tablespoons sugar

1½ cups light fruity Italian red wine such as Chianti, Lambrusco, Nebbiolo, or Valpolicella

Fresh mint leaves for garnish

Bring a large saucepan of water to a boil. Fill a large bowl with ice and water and place it near the stove.

Using a slotted spoon, lower the peaches into the boiling water and boil just until their skins begin to wrinkle, about 30 seconds. With the slotted spoon, transfer the peaches to the ice water and let them cool for a few minutes.

Drain the peaches and gently pat them dry with paper towels. Using a small, sharp knife, carefully peel the peaches. Cut them into halves, remove the stones, and cut into slices ½ to ¾ inch thick.

Put the peaches in a nonreactive mixing bowl. Sprinkle with the sugar and toss gently to combine. Pour in the wine, cover, and macerate in the refrigerator for 1 to 3 hours, gently stirring a few times. To serve, spoon the fruit and wine into attractive individual bowls and garnish with mint leaves.

Amaretto Peaches with Toasted Polenta Mascarpone Pound Cake

Think of this as a sophisticated yet easy Italian version of peach shortcake, great with coffee at the end of a meal or as a midmorning treat in its own right. Fresh summer peaches (or nectarines) are quickly sautéed with butter and a splash of the popular apricot-and-almond-flavored Italian liqueur, amaretto, then spooned over toasted slices of golden polenta pound cake.

MAKES 6 TO 12 SERVINGS

¾ cup slivered almonds

Polenta Mascarpone Pound Cake
(see Index)

Whipped Mascarpone Cream
(see Index)

6 large ripe but firm sweet
freestone peaches

4 tablespoons unsalted butter

6 tablespoons sugar

⅓ cup amaretto liqueur

Preheat the oven to 325°F and toast the almonds in a baking dish until golden, 5 to 7 minutes.

Prepare the pound cake and the mascarpone cream in advance. When the pound cake is cool, cut it crosswise into 12 equal slices. Arrange the slices on a baking sheet. Preheat the broiler.

Bring a large saucepan of water to a boil. Fill a large bowl with ice and water and place it near the stove.

Using a slotted spoon, lower the peaches into the boiling water and boil just until their skins begin to wrinkle, about 30 seconds. With the slotted spoon, transfer the peaches to the ice water and let them cool for a few minutes.

Drain the peaches and gently pat them dry with paper towels. Using a small, sharp knife, carefully peel the peaches. Cut them into halves, remove the stones, and cut into slices ½ to ¾ inch thick.

In a large skillet, melt the butter over medium heat. Add the peach slices, sugar, and amaretto and sauté, stirring frequently while taking care not to break up the peaches, until the fruit is heated through and a syrup has formed, 4 to 5 minutes.

Meanwhile, toast the pound cake slices under the broiler until light golden brown, 1 to 2 minutes per side; keep a careful eye on them so they don't burn.

As soon as the peaches and pound cake are ready, place one or two slices of the cake on each serving plate. Spoon the peaches and their sauce on top. Garnish with the Whipped Mascarpone Cream and toasted almonds and serve immediately.

Red and Green Grape Tart

When sweet seedless grapes are in the market, try using them as a filling for this simple tart, which makes a lovely conclusion served with good Italian-style coffee. Be as casual or precise as you like about the placement of the different-colored grapes, jumbling them all together as they fall into the shell or arranging them carefully in concentric circles, precise wedges, or other patterns. Serve the tart warm or at room temperature.

MAKES 1 9-INCH TART; 6 TO 8 SERVINGS

Basic Tart Pastry (see Index)	¾ pound seedless red grapes,
2 extra-large egg yolks	stemmed (about 2 cups)
¼ cup heavy cream	¾ pound seedless green grapes,
2 tablespoons light brown sugar	stemmed (about 2 cups)
2 tablespoons grappa (Italian	2 tablespoons granulated sugar
brandy, optional)	⅓ cup slivered almonds or pine nuts

Preheat the oven to 425°F.

On a lightly floured work surface, use a rolling pin to roll out the pastry dough into an even circle 12 inches in diameter. Loosely roll up the circle around the rolling pin, transfer it to a 9-inch tart pan with a removable bottom, and unroll. With your fingers, gently press the dough into the pan. Use a small, sharp knife to carefully trim the dough even with the edge of the pan.

With a fork, prick the dough's bottom and sides all over. Tear off a 24-inch-long sheet of aluminum foil, fold it in half, poke a few holes in it, and press it down inside the tart pan to cover the dough. Bake for 8 minutes, then remove the foil and continue baking until the pastry looks dry and firm but not yet brown, about 4 minutes more. Remove the pan from the oven. Reduce the oven temperature to 325°F.

In a mixing bowl, use a wire whisk or electric mixer on low speed to blend together the egg yolks, cream, brown sugar, and, if you like, the grappa. Pour the mixture into the tart shell.

Arrange the grapes in the tart shell, pressing them gently into the egg mixture. Sprinkle evenly with the granulated sugar.

Put the tart in the oven and bake until the grapes are bubbling and the edges of the tart are golden brown, 35 to 40 minutes. If the pastry appears to be browning too quickly, shield the edges by covering them with strips of aluminum foil, placed shiny side out.

When the tart is done, transfer it to a wire rack to cool for about 15 minutes. Meanwhile, spread the almonds or pine nuts in a baking dish and toast them in the oven until golden, 5 to 7 minutes. Strew them over the surface of the tart.

To unmold, place the tart on top of a plate smaller than its bottom or on top of a wide can; then gently pull down its side, using a knife tip to loosen the edges of the pastry if necessary. Cut into wedges and serve.

Fresh Cherry-Chocolate-Hazelnut Tart with Frangelico

Frangelico, an Italian liqueur made from wild hazelnuts and herbs, gives an intriguing extra dimension of flavor to the fresh, ripe cherries that fill this casual yet very sophisticated fruit tart, perfect to serve with coffee at the end of a special brunch. If you like, however, you may omit the Frangelico and still have a delicious, attractive effect. For an even more eye-catching look, use a mixture of different sweet cherry types, perhaps combining deep red Bing cherries with the yellow-orange Rainier variety.

MAKES 1 9-INCH TART; 6 TO 8 SERVINGS

1½ pounds plump ripe sweet cherries, pitted

¼ cup Frangelico

Basic Tart Pastry (see Index)

⅓ cup hazelnuts

6 ounces semisweet chocolate, broken into pieces

1 cup mascarpone, at room temperature

Preheat the oven to 425°F.

Put the pitted cherries in a mixing bowl and toss with the Frangelico. Cover and refrigerate, stirring occasionally, for 1 to 2 hours.

Meanwhile, on a lightly floured work surface, use a rolling pin to roll out the pastry dough into an even circle 12 inches in diameter. Loosely roll up the circle around the rolling pin, transfer it to a 9-inch tart pan with a removable bottom, and unroll. With your fingers, gently press the dough into the pan. Use a small, sharp knife to carefully trim the dough even with the edge of the pan.

With a fork, prick the dough's bottom and sides all over. Tear off a 24-inch-long sheet of aluminum foil, fold it in half, poke a few holes in it, and press it down inside the tart pan to cover the dough. Bake for 4 minutes. Remove the foil and continue baking until the pastry looks crisp and golden brown, 8 to 10 minutes more. Transfer the pastry to a wire rack to cool.

Spread the hazelnuts in a baking dish and toast them in the oven until golden, 3 to 5 minutes. Remove them from the heat and, while they are still warm, fold them inside a kitchen towel and rub to remove their skins. (Empty the skins from the towel into the kitchen sink.) Transfer the nuts to a bowl and leave to cool. Then put them in a food processor with the metal blade and pulse several times until coarsely chopped.

To assemble the tart, put the chocolate pieces in the top half of a double boiler over but not touching simmering water. Stir until the chocolate melts. Spoon the chocolate into the cooled tart shell, using the back of the spoon to smooth it evenly. Immediately sprinkle with the chopped hazelnuts and leave until the chocolate has set. Spoon the cherries into the shell. Transfer the mascarpone to a small serving bowl with a spoon.

To unmold, place the tart on top of a plate smaller than its bottom or on top of a wide can; then gently pull down its side, using a knife tip to loosen the edges of the pastry if necessary. Cut into wedges and serve, passing mascarpone to spoon over individual servings.

Summer Fruit with Lemon Panna Cotta

To conclude a brunch on a hot summer weekend, this cooling Italian dessert makes quite an impression. Panna cotta literally means "cooked cream," referring to the brief heating of the cream before it is combined with the gelatin that sets it to a smooth, soothing, custardlike consistency—a perfect foil to summer's sweet, colorful, juicy fruit. Relatively easy to prepare, the panna cotta can be made the night before, ready to unmold and arrange with the fruit just before serving.

MAKES 6 SERVINGS

½ cup whole milk
1 tablespoon unflavored gelatin
    powder
2½ cups heavy cream
6 tablespoons sugar

2 tablespoons grated lemon zest
1 teaspoon vanilla extract
4½ cups mixed whole berries or
    sliced peaches, nectarines,
    or plums

Put the milk in a large heatproof mixing bowl. Sprinkle the gelatin powder over it and leave it to soften.

Meanwhile, in a saucepan, stir together the cream, sugar, and lemon zest. Place over medium heat and cook, stirring occasionally, until the sugar dissolves and the cream just begins to simmer.

Stirring the gelatin-milk mixture continuously with a whisk, slowly pour in the hot cream mixture. Stir in the vanilla. With a ladle, divide the mixture evenly among six ¾-cup custard cups or ramekins. Cover with plastic wrap and transfer to the refrigerator to chill until set, 3 hours to overnight.

Just before serving, loosen the panna cotta in each cup by running a small knife around its side. Turn each cup over onto the center of a chilled serving plate, tap gently to dislodge the panna cotta, and lift the cup away. Arrange the fruit around the panna cotta and serve immediately.

Herbed Mushroom Sauté and Broiled Tomatoes with Herbed Parmesan Bread Crumb Stuffing

Herbed Mushroom Sauté

Mushrooms are my favorite morning vegetable, providing robust counterpoints of flavor and texture to egg dishes and sausages or ham. The key to success with this dish lies in using a large, heavy skillet that conducts heat well; otherwise the mushrooms will release their juices instead of browning quickly. Use the smallest mushrooms you can find in the produce department or farmer's market. Try brown-skinned cremini mushrooms along with or in place of the regular white cultivated ones.

MAKES 6 TO 8 SERVINGS

3 tablespoons extra-virgin olive oil
3 tablespoons unsalted butter
2 shallots, minced
1½ pounds small mushrooms,
    brushed clean, stems trimmed
1 tablespoon fresh lemon juice

3 tablespoons finely shredded
    fresh basil
3 tablespoons finely chopped fresh
    Italian parsley
Salt
Freshly ground black pepper

In a large, heavy skillet, heat the olive oil and butter over medium-high heat. Add the shallots and, as soon as they sizzle, raise the heat to high and add the mushrooms. Stir the mushrooms continuously until they are tender and just beginning to brown slightly, 4 to 5 minutes. Sprinkle with lemon juice, scatter with basil and parsley, season lightly with salt and pepper, and stir briefly. Transfer to a heated serving dish and serve immediately.

Broiled Tomatoes with Herbed Parmesan Bread Crumb Stuffing

Quickly prepared, these make a colorful and flavorful accompaniment to egg dishes, sausages, and bacon. They work well on a buffet, too, since they continue to look and taste good even as they cool to room temperature. Get the crumbs from a good-quality rustic Italian-style or sourdough loaf.

MAKES 4 TO 8 SERVINGS

4 large firm Roma (plum) tomatoes
1 cup coarse fresh white bread crumbs
½ cup freshly grated Parmesan cheese
6 tablespoons unsalted butter, melted
2 tablespoons finely shredded fresh basil

2 tablespoons finely chopped fresh chives
2 tablespoons finely chopped fresh Italian parsley
1 teaspoon dried oregano, crumbled
Salt
Freshly ground black pepper

Preheat the broiler and place the rack 8 to 10 inches away from the heat.

Meanwhile, with the tip of a small, sharp knife, cut out the cores from the tomatoes. Cut each tomato in half lengthwise, through its core and stem ends. With a fingertip, hollow out each tomato half, removing and discarding the watery seed sacs and the thin walls of flesh between them.

In a mixing bowl, combine the bread crumbs, Parmesan cheese, melted butter, and herbs. Season to taste with salt and black pepper and stir until well mixed. Spoon the mixture into the tomato halves, packing it in well and mounding it smoothly.

Lightly grease a baking dish large enough to hold all the tomatoes and place the tomatoes in it, stuffing up. Broil them until the stuffing is golden brown and the tomatoes are hot, 5 to 7 minutes. Serve from the baking dish or transfer to individual serving plates.

Rosemary-Parmesan Rösti

The traditional shredded potato cake of Switzerland works spectacularly as a morning side dish with scrambled or fried eggs and your favorite breakfast meats. A hint of rosemary and a layer of shaved Parmesan add an extra dimension to the potatoes. You can make this dish up to several hours ahead of time, leaving it in the pan, covered, at room temperature and then reheating it at 350°F for about 5 minutes.

MAKES 6 TO 8 SERVINGS

1½ pounds baking potatoes
2 teaspoons dried rosemary,
    crumbled
½ teaspoon salt

2 tablespoons unsalted butter
1 tablespoon extra-virgin olive oil
½ cup freshly grated Parmesan
    cheese

Preheat the oven to 450°F.

Peel the potatoes and shred them with the coarse shredding disk of a food processor or the large holes of a box shredder/grater. In a mixing bowl, toss the shreds with the rosemary and salt.

In a 9- or 10-inch nonstick ovenproof skillet, heat the butter with the olive oil over medium heat. Spread one-third of the potatoes in an even layer in the skillet and sprinkle with half of the Parmesan. Top with another third of the potatoes, then the remaining Parmesan and the remaining potatoes.

Fry undisturbed until the edges of the potatoes begin to brown, about 5 minutes. Transfer the skillet to the oven and bake until the underside of the rösti is a deep golden brown, about 40 minutes, using a spatula to lift the edge of the cake gently to check toward the end of the cooking time.

Remove the skillet from the oven and use a spatula to loosen its edges all around. Invert a heatproof serving platter over the skillet. Using pot holders or oven mitts, carefully hold the skillet and the platter together and invert them to unmold the rösti onto the platter. Cut into wedges and serve immediately.

INDEX